Acknowledgements

I would like to thank Tina Brookes, Sinead Corry, Susan Lewry, Sue Long, Adam Piper, Abigail Parr and David Miller for their dedicated help and support.

Thanks also to Malcolm, and our families, for tasting so many new recipes, always with some degree of enthusiasm!

To save on paper and production costs, this book was limited to 96 pages of text.

Three full bonus recipes are available by e-mailing Beverley at

Beverley.piper@jarvishomes.com

Also by Beverley Piper

Fast and Healthy Family cookery
Beverley Piper's Quick and Easy Healthy Cookery
Super Juice
Super Juice for Slimmers
The Daily Express Entertaining in a Flash
The Daily Express Family food in a Flash

Menu 17

Beverley Piper

Introduction

"Staying in is the new going out," and is a great idea, as it avoids paying for some of those expensive restaurant meals.

Cooking for friends is making quite a comeback and this book aims to help you save money by eating well at home, using seasonal, inexpensive ingredients.

Having lived through more than one recession and worked as a home economist for over 40 years, I have penned some of my popular recipes, which hopefully, will be much used.

Most of us enjoy welcoming family and friends into our homes. We just need a bit of help with the food!

These 21 menus, each with a useful time plan and set of hints and tips, are varied in content and cost and have been planned for different occasions.

You will notice that some luxury ingredients, such as wine, butter, cream, chocolate, etc., have been included. This book, is for "entertaining" and a little of these special ingredients, quickly changes a mundane dish into something sensational.

INGREDIENTS and STORE CUPBOARD

It is easier to cook if you keep a well-managed store cupboard, equipped with basic foods.

LIST OF STAPLES

Sugar: Caster, icing, Demerara.

Flour etc: Cornflour, self raising, plain, wholemeal or seed and grain bread flour, cocoa powder, bicarbonate of soda, cream of tartar.

Dried herbs and spices: Parsley, coriander, mixed herbs, coriander seeds, cumin seeds, medium hot curry powder, sea salt, black pepper corns, smoked paprika, ground cinnamon, cinnamon sticks, garam masala, cloves, blackened Cajun seasoning.

Vinegars: White and red wine vinegar, balsamic vinegar.

Fresh garlic cloves.

Oils: olive, extra virgin olive, sesame, sunflower, vegetable or corn oil.

Nuts: Brazil, pine nut kernels.

Seeds: pumpkin seeds, sesame seeds.

Stock cubes: lamb, beef and chicken, Swiss vegetable bouillon powder.

Mustard: Dijon, wholegrain, English.

Sauces, etc: Runny honey, lemon curd, tomato ketchup, Worcestershire sauce, redcurrant jelly, fish sauce, mayonnaise, truly lazy chillies.

Cans: chopped tomatoes, ready made custard, coconut milk, condensed milk, tuna fish.

Rice, Grains and Pasta: Couscous, Basmati and long grain rice, spaghetti, lasagne sheets.

Chocolate: good quality cooking chocolate. I recommend Green and Blacks.

PLANNING YOUR PARTY

Remember, menus are for 6 people, except for the Buffet, menu 11, which serves 8-10. Select a menu that will fit into your schedule.

For ease and speed, remember to plan, preparing a detailed list before you shop. Also aim to do at least some preparation and cooking in advance.

Purchase most necessary items under one roof, or make use of internet shopping and home delivery, to save you time and money.

DRINKS

Offer a selection of chilled non-alcoholic drinks, plus water, both still and sparkling.

A WORD ABOUT WINE

Allow about ½ bottle of wine per person plus an aperitif. A wine bottle is 750 ml, thus serving between 4-6 glasses.

For pre-dinner tipples, I have included a couple of our favourite recipes.

SUMMER PARTY PITCHERS

The Sun lounger

In a large jug, mix 150ml of cranberry juice, 300ml grapefruit juice and 100ml peach purée, (canned peaches are fine, drained and blitzed in a food processor.)
Add 100ml white rum and plenty of ice cubes. Top up with lemonade. Stir before serving with slices of orange, nectarine or peach. Prefer a non-alcoholic punch? Leave out the rum!

Who's For a Jeeves?

Fill a large jug one third full of Jeeves, a great tasting, alcoholic mixer drink available at a very reasonable price! Cram the jug full of ice cubes and add sliced strawberries, orange, apple, and cucumber. Top up with diet lemonade or tonic water. Stir well. Add sprigs of mint and serve.

Mulled Wine

Pour 2 litres of red wine into a large pan. Add 600ml orange juice, and 300ml water. Stir in 200g caster sugar. Add 1 cinnamon stick. Stud 1 large lemon and 1 large orange with cloves. Add to pan. Heat together slowly, stirring until sugar melts. Simmer very gently, covered, for 1 hour. Serve warm.

PRE-DINNER NIBBLES

Offer two types of ripe melon, (Charentais and Galia look nice), with sliced nectarine and peach, all arranged on a large platter.

Try slices of smoked salmon spread with cream cheese, rolled and secured with cocktail sticks. Good quality pesto stirred into Greek yoghurt, (approximately ½ jar pesto to 200g yoghurt) and taramasalata; make good dips, served with vegetable sticks, or warm pitta bread. The easy guacamole recipe on page 78 is delicious, served as a dip.

HINTS & TIPS

- Fill empty, used dishes with cold water immediately, to ease washing up.
- Check plates, cutlery, glasses and all equipment needed, in advance, to ensure you have sufficient. Allow at least 2 glasses per person as people tend to put glasses down and lose them! Large supermarkets hire glasses free of charge, requiring only a small deposit.
- Use microwave and freezer, where appropriate. Both will save you time and effort.
- Assemble all serving dishes and plates and warm before use, even if it means simply rinsing in very hot water.
- Ensure you have sufficient oven space to cook and keep dishes warm. Don't cram the oven full as air must be allowed to circulate for efficiency.
- Consider fridge space, especially in summer. You may need to chill several dishes as well as bottles of wine. A large cool box is useful for chilling white wine and water.
- Check jugs for water; ice cubes which can be bought in the supermarket, chairs and table cloths or mats.
- Invest in a meat thermometer. This handy, inexpensive piece of equipment is inserted into roast meats and poultry, and indicates when they are cooked.
- A simple way to round off a meal is a well-presented cheese board. Arrange 3 or 4 varieties of cheese with a selection of biscuits, grapes and celery. Fresh slices of peach and mango, figs, chutney and pickle are good accompaniments.
- Chocolates – should you not wish to serve a dessert, hand around a selection of chocolates, both plain, milk and white to finish off the meal.
- As today more and more people avoid coffee, offer a selection of different teas as an alternative.

NB: Before making any recipe in this book, assemble all ingredients and equipment on your work top. This simple action will make life easier saving you time and frustration.

All spoons measures are to British Standards and should be level unless otherwise stated.

All timings in Time Plans are approximate.

Ovens and grills must be preheated to specified temperature before cooking.

COOKING CONVERSIONS FOR AMERICA
Please note that all measurements are approximate.

AMERICAN LIQUID MEASURES
1 Cup	= 275ml
1 Pint	= 550ml
1 Quart	= 900ml
1 ½ Cups	= ½ pint
2 ½ Cups	= 1 pint
3 ¾ Cups	= 1 ½ pints

AMERICAN SOLID MEASURES
1 Cup Rice	= 225g
1 Cup Flour	= 115g
¼ Cup Flour	= 25g
1 Cup Butter	= 225g
1 Stick Butter	= 115g
1 Cup Brown Sugar	= 180g
1 Cup Granulated Sugar	= 225g
1 Cup Dried Fruit	= 225g

for courgettes, use zucchini
for aubergine, use egg plant
for spring onions, use scallions
for peeled prawns, use shelled shrimps
for stock, use bouillon
for double cream, use heavy cream
for tomato purée, use tomato paste

CREDIT CRUNCH KNOW HOW

- Freeze left over wine in ice cube trays. Bag up, label and freeze. Use in cooking, at a later date.
- Crumb day old bread in food processor. Bag up, label and freeze. Invaluable for use as toppings and coatings. Can be used from frozen.
- Make use of left overs. For a wonderful soup, simmer left-over vegetables in stock, for about 15 minutes. Whiz to blend, adding a little cream, if available, and maybe some freshly chopped herbs. Serve piping hot.
- Left over meat and fish can be diced and added, with a little stock, to cooked rice for a speedy lunch, or combined with a sauce and tossed with cooked pasta for a filling supper dish.
- Grow herbs, either on the windowsill or in the garden. Freeze fresh herbs, when in season, for winter use. Far cheaper and more convenient than those little bags of herbs, sold in supermarkets.
- Olive oil, although delicious, is expensive. Flavour vegetable oil by adding a sprig of rosemary and a couple of bay leaves to the bottle. Store in larder. An excellent alternative to olive oil for use in dressings and cooking.
- Buy salmon when on offer, usually at Easter and Christmas. Purchase the whole fish, asking the fishmonger to cut it into steaks or fillets for you, or do it your self, at home. Pack, label and freeze fish that you are not going to use immediately.
- Frozen meat and fish are normally cheaper than fresh and usually very good. Look out for offers. Defrost over night, in the fridge, before using in recipes.
- Buy fruits such as raspberries, cherries, plums and red currants when in season or pick your own from the farm. Bag up, label and freeze for winter use.
- Avoid bags of pre-washed mixed salad leaves, which are treated with chemicals, to prolong life. Instead, purchase a couple of different varieties of whole lettuces. The lettuces will last longer and taste superior.
- Avoid pre-packed vegetables as they tend to "sweat" in their packaging and don't last long. Instead buy vegetables loose. Transfer, unpacked, to chill drawer of fridge, for storage.
- Combine a small amount of grated Parmesan cheese, in a bag, with ordinary Cheddar. The Cheddar quickly absorbs the flavour of the more expensive Parmesan.

Menu 2

Menu 20

Menu 19

Menu List

Menu 1   Page 14
Birthday Celebration Lunch or Dinner
Garlic Mushrooms
Spiced Rack of Lamb with Red Wine Gravy & Butternut Squash Purée
Buttered New Potatoes with Fresh Herbs
Lemon Syllabub with Raspberries

Menu 2   Page 18
Supper for Family and/or Friends
Asian Style Smoked Salmon with Bean Sprout & Coriander Salad
Chicken & Broccoli Bake
Roasted Roots
Flapjack and Raspberry Trifle

Menu 3   Page 22
Bank Holiday Week End Lunch
Butternut Squash & Onion Soup
Marinated Tuna
Red & Green Coleslaw
New Potatoes with Butter & Herbs
Stuffed Mushrooms
Plum and Blackberry Crumble and/or Poached Pears

Menu 4   Page 28
New Year's Eve Supper
Parma Ham with Fresh Pear & Dolcellata
Hungarian Goulash with Jacket Potatoes
Dressed Mixed Salad
Eton Mess

Menu 5   Page 32
Speedy Light Lunch
Sesame Salmon with Crème Fraiche Sauce, Roast Tomatoes & Noodles
Salad with Feta Cheese
Strawberries Dipped in Chocolate

Menu 6   Page 36
Supper for Friends
Carrot & Parsnip Soup
Spicy Shepherd's Pie
Roast Carrots & Courgettes
Mango Melon & Ginger Fruit Salad

Menu 7   Page 40
Easter Sunday Lunch
Herbed Roast Shoulder Lamb
Mange-Tout & Carrots with Sage & Lemon Butter
Roasted New Potatoes with Salsa
Baked White Chocolate Cheesecake with Strawberries

Menu 8   Page 44
Delicious Weekend Menu
Fish Pie with Salmon, Prawns & Dill
Cauliflower & Broccoli
Decadent Chocolate Cake

Menu 9   Page 48
Family Supper
Chilli Con Carne
Garlic Bread
Easy Apple Tarts
Chocolate Mousse

Menu 10   Page 52
Classic Italian
Mussels with Garlic & Cream
Beef Lasagne
Ciabatta Bread Salad
Zabaglione

Menu 11   Page 56
Plan in advance Buffet Dinner Party
Whole Baked Salmon with Dill
Pork & Chorizo Stew
Spinach & Avocado Salad
Lemon, Raspberry & Kiwifruit Pavlova

Menu 12   Page 62
Slow Cooked Lunch or Supper
Roast Belly of Pork with Roast Apples, Onions & Cider Gravy
Mashed Potatoes
Buttery Cabbage with Caraway Seeds
Steamed Syrup Sponge

Menu 13   Page 66
Entertain from the Freezer
Chicken Liver Pâté
Lamb Hot Pot with Sweet Potato Mash
Lemon Cheesecake

Menu 14   Page 70
Celebration Dinner Party
Easy Carbonara
Steamed Broccoli & Asparagus
Chocolate Biscuit Cake
Sliced Melon with Blackberries

Menu 15   Page 72
Saturday Lunch or Supper
Sausage Casserole
Potatoes Dauphinoise with Onion
Swede & Carrot Crush
Crème Brulée

Menu 16   Page 76
Teenagers Party
Cajun Chicken Fajitas
Easy Guacamole
Cherry Clafoutis

Menu 17   Page 80
Vegetarian
Sweet Potato, Mozzarella & Pesto Tart
Soda Bread
Jelly Trifles

Menu 18   Page 84
Entertaining in a Flash
Oven-Fried Indian Chicken
Minty Little Gem & Tomato Salad
Fruits in Kirsch

Menu 19   Page 86
One Pot Supper
Lamb Tagine
Couscous
Lemon Meringue Pie

Menu 20 Page 90
Festive Buffet
Cider Baked Gammon
Cheddar Cheese & Broccoli Flan
New Potatoes
Coleslaw with Blue Cheese Dressing
Banoffi Pie

Menu 21 Page 94
Quick and Easy Supper
Chicken and Mushroom Risotto
Griddled Pineapple with Blackberries

Menu 1

MENU 1
Birthday Celebration Lunch or Dinner
Serves 6
A little effort needed: Ready in 1 hour approx.

* Garlic Mushrooms
* Spiced Rack of Lamb with Red Wine Gravy & Butternut Squash Purée
* Buttered New Potatoes with Fresh Herbs
* Lemon Syllabub with Raspberries

Try to buy the lamb, trimmed, from your local butcher. It is often cheaper than supermarkets.

A little red wine is used in the gravy and white wine is an ingredient of syllabub. Buy wines for both recipes, in the supermarket, serving remainder, at correct temperature, to drink with the meal. Supermarkets now all have reputable wine buyers and most of their wine choices can be depended upon.

This is a straight forward menu to prepare and cook.

The lamb can be coated with the rub, in the morning, and chilled. For superb flavour, remember to take lamb out of fridge 30 minutes before cooking so that it reaches room temperature.

A good way of cooking new potatoes is to simmer in boiling water, until almost tender (about 16 minutes) then leave covered, towards back of stove, still in water but with heat switched off. They will "hold" like this for up to 45 minutes and be perfect when drained to serve!

COOK'S HINTS & TIPS
Prepare syllabub up to 4 hours ahead and chill.
The butternut squash purée freezes well. De-frost overnight in refrigerator.
To re-heat from defrosted: either cover with cling film and microwave for 4-5 minutes, stirring halfway through or cover with foil and re-heat in oven, below lamb, for approx. 40 minutes. Stir well before serving piping hot.
Allowing lamb to "rest" for 15 minutes before carving will improve both flavour and texture of the meat.
The mushrooms are very quick and easy to cook at the last minute.

SIMPLE TIME PLAN
To eat at: **8.15pm**
During Morning Prepare syllabub and chill in fridge.
Prepare and cook butternut squash purée.
Cool, cover and chill.
Chop herbs for potatoes.
Chill in airtight container in fridge.

6.45pm	Pre-heat oven, to 220C (200 fan), Gas 7.
	Prepare lamb with rub and set aside in kitchen.
7.00pm	Re-heat butternut squash purée, if using oven.
	Put lamb in pre-heated oven.
7.15pm	Cook the potatoes.
	Simply cover 1kg washed new potatoes with cold water, cutting large potatoes in half.
	Add ½ teaspoon salt, cover and bring to the boil.
	Simmer 15-20 minutes until tender.
	Drain and return to pan.
	Add a knob of unsalted butter and a large handful of herbs of your choice.
	Toss gently.
	Turn into warmed vegetable tureen and serve, or cover and keep warm until service.
	Any fresh herbs will do but a mixture of chopped parsley, chives and tarragon are nice.
7.30pm	Remove lamb from oven and set aside to rest.
	Make gravy.
	Keep warm.
7.55pm	If using microwave: re-heat butternut squash purée.
	Note: If butternut squash purée is in the conventional oven, turn temperature down to low.
8.00pm	Cook mushroom starter.

GARLIC MUSHROOM STARTER

The soda bread from menu 17 goes well with the mushrooms.
Use a box of value button mushrooms, available in most supermarkets, for this recipe.

175g smoked streaky bacon, de-rinded
700g large button mushrooms, cleaned
4 tablespoons olive oil
50g butter
3 cloves garlic, chopped
Freshly ground black pepper
2 tablespoons freshly chopped parsley

Roughly chop bacon. Roughly chop mushrooms. They need to be in chunky pieces.
Heat a large, heavy based frying pan or wok and fry bacon until fat runs.
Increase heat and continue to fry until bacon crisps.
Remove bacon using a slotted spoon, drain on kitchen paper and keep warm.
Add oil and butter to the pan and heat until butter melts and foams.
Add mushrooms and cook over medium heat, for 3-4 minutes, stirring until mushrooms are tender. Add garlic and a seasoning of pepper. Return bacon to the pan.
Continue to cook for 1 minute.
Add parsley and toss to mix.
Divide mushroom mixture between ramekins or plates.

Serve immediately, accompanied by slices of soda bread.

SPICED RACK OF LAMB WITH BUTTERNUT SQUASH PURÉE

Easy: Ready in 50 minutes, approx, plus resting time

½ tablespoon coriander seeds
½ tablespoon cumin seeds
1 clove garlic, crushed
2 tablespoons olive oil
2 racks lamb, each with 8 bones, French trimmed

For the Butternut Squash Purée:
1kg butternut squash, peeled and chopped, discarding seeds
25g butter
Grated rind and strained juice ½ small orange
Salt & black pepper
1 tablespoon freshly chopped parsley

Crush together, in a pestle and mortar, coriander and cumin seeds.
Alternatively use a Pyrex bowl and the end of a rolling pin.
Add garlic and olive oil. Mix to a paste. Add a seasoning of salt and pepper.
Rub this spicy mixture all over lamb. Set aside for 30 minutes, or chill in the fridge for several hours.
Pre-heat oven to 220C (200 fan), Gas 7.
Place lamb, which must be at room temperature before cooking, into roasting tin.
Cook for approximately 35-40 minutes for pink, a little longer if you prefer your meat medium. Allow to rest for 15 minutes before carving.

Meanwhile, steam or simmer butternut squash in a little boiling water, for about 20 minutes, until tender. Drain if necessary. Mash well using a potato masher, adding butter, orange rind and juice and a seasoning of salt and pepper.
Add parsley and turn into warmed vegetable tureen to serve.

WINE GRAVY

150ml red wine
450ml lamb stock
4 teaspoons cornflour
30ml redcurrant jelly
1 teaspoon tomato sauce

Transfer cooked lamb to a warmed carving platter. Cover with foil and set aside in a warm place to rest.
Transfer any sediment and fat left in roasting tin to a saucepan (you are far less likely to get lumps this way!) Add red wine and lamb stock. Bring to boil, then simmer for 10 minutes. Remove pan from heat. Set aside for 5 minutes to cool a little.
In a mug, mix cornflour to a smooth paste with a little cold water. Stir into stock mixture.
Bring pan to the boil, slowly, stirring constantly until a perfect gravy results. Stir in redcurrant jelly and tomato sauce. Continue to simmer gently for 3-4 minutes.
Serve.

LEMON SYLLABUB WITH RASPBERRIES

Easy: Ready in 15 minutes approx, plus chilling time.

200ml fruity medium white wine such as German Riesling
Grated rind and strained juice of 1 large lemon
50g caster sugar
450ml double cream
225g fresh raspberries

Put wine, lemon rind and juice into a large mixing bowl. Add sugar and double cream. Whisk using electric beaters until light and creamy. It will soon thicken to the consistency of whipped cream.
Divide raspberries between 6 stemmed wine glasses. Spoon syllabub, evenly, over fruit. Chill for at least 10 minutes before serving.
Note
Try to make this dessert in the morning and serve at dinner. Just cover with cling film and store in fridge.

MENU 2
Supper for Family and/or Friends
An excellent menu for those organised folk who prefer to "get ahead"
Serves 6
Some skill needed: Ready in 3 hours approx.

* Asian Style Smoked Salmon with Bean Sprout & Coriander Salad
* Chicken & Broccoli Bake
* Roasted Roots
* Flapjack & Raspberry Trifle

COOK'S HINTS AND TIPS

Aim to prepare both the trifle and the chicken & broccoli bake during the morning.

Cool chicken bake. Chill both dishes, covered with cling film. Remove chicken bake from fridge and leave at room temperature for 30 minutes before baking.

Try to find supermarket's finest flapjack for the trifle as they are normally very good.

SIMPLE TIME PLAN

To eat at: **8pm assuming you are using only one oven.**
N.B Both the chicken & broccoli bake and the roasted roots will be cooked together, using good oven management!
Pre-heat oven, to 220C (fan 200), Gas 7. When vegetables have had 30 minutes in centre of oven, transfer vegetables to top of oven and reduce temperature to 190°C (170 fan), Gas 5.
Add chicken & broccoli bake to centre of oven and continue to cook both dishes, for 30-35 minutes, until vegetables are tinged golden and chicken & broccoli bake is crisp and golden.

5pm	Prepare roasted roots. Toss ingredients together in roasting tin. Set aside.
5.25pm	Prepare trifle and chill.
6.00pm	Prepare chicken & broccoli dish. Pre-heat oven to 220C (200 fan), Gas 7.
6.45pm	Prepare smoked salmon starter. Chill until ready to serve.
	Store the bean sprout salad, covered, in the fridge. Don't open the packet of smoked salmon until ready to plate up.
7.00pm	Cook roasted veg.
7.30pm	Bake chicken dish, turning oven down.
7.35pm	Assemble starter and put in place on the table.
7.45pm	Enjoy a drink with your guests
8.00pm	Sit down for starter. Check oven and turn to low. Bon appétit!

ASIAN STYLE SMOKED SALMON WITH BEANSPROUT & CORIANDER SALAD

Easy: Ready in 15 minutes approx

Serve with a basket of walnut bread or rye bread, sliced at the last minute.

300g smoked salmon
75g bean sprouts
8 cherry tomatoes, halved
8 radishes, washed and sliced
1 bunch fresh coriander, finely chopped
1 mild red chilli, de-seeded and finely sliced

For the dressing
4 tablespoons extra virgin olive oil
Grated rind and strained juice 1 lime
1 teaspoon fish sauce
1 teaspoon caster sugar
1 small clove garlic, chopped
Salt & black pepper

Start by sharing the smoked salmon between 6 side plates, use plain white plates, if possible.

In a salad bowl, combine bean sprouts, tomatoes, radishes, coriander and chilli. Prepare dressing. Combine ingredients for dressing in a screw top jar. Shake to combine. Taste and adjust seasoning, if required. Remember the chilli and only use a little pepper, if any.

When ready to serve, pour dressing over salad ingredients and toss to coat. Arrange a small pile of salad, beside smoked salmon, on each plate. Serve immediately, accompanied by the bread.

CHICKEN & BROCCOLI BAKE

A little effort: 40 minutes approx

The sauce is made by an easy, one stage method and is absolutely foolproof. It may take a little longer than the conventional method but it never goes lumpy!
The Stilton cheese gives a delicious "bite" to this dish but if preferred leave it out and use 50g Cheddar cheese instead.

3 tablespoons corn or vegetable oil
6 large chicken breast fillets
225g broccoli florettes
50g butter
30g plain flour
Salt & black pepper
600ml whole or semi skimmed milk
1 tablespoon Dijon mustard

For the topping
3 slices from a large wholemeal cut loaf, crusts removed
25g mature Cheddar cheese, roughly chopped
25g Stilton cheese, crumbled

Heat the oil in a large, non-stick frying pan. Fry diced chicken for about 10 minutes, turning frequently, until golden on all sides. Drain on absorbent kitchen paper and set aside.

Cook broccoli in a little boiling water for about 3-5 minutes. Alternatively, steam broccoli, for about 6 minutes, until just tender.
Turn broccoli into a sieve and pass under running, cold water.
This will immediately stop the cooking process. Drain well and set aside.

Make the sauce. In a large, non-stick saucepan, put butter, flour, and a seasoning of salt and pepper. Add milk. Stand pan over a moderate heat, whisking continuously with a balloon whisk, until mixture boils and a creamy, thickened sauce results, about 8 minutes.

Lower heat and continue to simmer for 5 minutes, stirring now and again.
Remove from heat. Stir mustard into the sauce, stir in chicken and broccoli.
Turn contents of pan into a gratin dish.

Prepare the topping. Tear bread into pieces and put into food processor fitted with the metal blade. Add cheese. Process until bread is crumbed and cheese is finely chopped.

When ready to cook, pre-heat oven to, 190C (170 fan), Gas 5. Sprinkle topping evenly over chicken dish. Bake in centre of oven for 30-35 minutes, until crisp and golden.
Serve.

ROASTED ROOTS

Easy: Ready in 1 hour 15 minutes approx

6 medium carrots, peeled and thickly sliced on the slant
4 medium parsnips, peeled and sliced, discarding woody stems
4 medium red-skinned potatoes cut into wedges
3 red-skinned onions, peeled and cut into wedges
2 celery stalks, sliced
2 yellow peppers, sliced
2 cloves garlic, crushed
1 large courgette, sliced fairly thickly
2 teaspoons dried mixed herbs or 2 tablespoons freshly chopped herbs of your choice
3 tablespoons olive oil
Salt & black pepper

Put prepared vegetables into a very large, heavy based roasting tin. Add garlic, herbs and oil.

Season with a little salt and pepper. Using two large spoons, toss everything together. If preferred, this preparation can be done two hours ahead of cooking. Simply cover with cling film and chill until ready to cook.

Pre-heat oven to 220C (200 fan), Gas 7. Cook vegetables in centre of oven for about 55 minutes, stirring a couple of times. Keep your eye on them.

The vegetables are ready when lovely and golden and smelling wonderful!
Serve immediately.

FLAPJACK & RASPBERRY TRIFLE

Easy: 30 minutes approx

If the trifle is to be served to children, use red grape juice to soak flapjack, instead of Grand Marnier or whisky. You may prefer to spoon a little caster sugar over the raspberries before adding the custard.

8 flapjacks, supermarket's finest would be perfect
8 tablespoons Grand Marnier or whisky
450g fresh or frozen raspberries, or freshly stoned dark cherries, de-frosted, if frozen
2 x 425g cans ready-made custard (I like Ambrosia)
275ml double cream, whipped

To serve: a few raspberries or cherries

Break flapjack into pieces and lay in base of a large glass bowl.
Spoon Grand Marnier, evenly, over flapjack. Top with raspberries, or cherries.
Pour custard over to cover fruit. Carefully pour whipped cream on top of custard.
Chill in fridge until ready to serve.
Serve, decorated with the raspberries, or cherries.

MENU 3
Bank Holiday Weekend Lunch
Serves 6
Some skill required: Ready in 1 hour 30 minutes approx.

Although fresh tuna is not a particularly cheap fish, it is quick and easy to cook and truly impressive and delicious. For a more economical alternative, use salmon steaks and cook for about 3 minutes each side.
You may like to include the salad with feta cheese from menu 5.

* Butternut Squash & Onion Soup
* Marinated Tuna
* Red & Green Coleslaw
* New Potatoes with Butter & Herbs (see menu 1)
* Stuffed Mushrooms
* Plum and Blackberry Crumble and / or Poached Pears

COOK'S HINTS AND TIPS
No one wants to spend a long time slaving over a hot stove during the Bank Holiday so try to prepare much of this menu in advance. The soup and crumble both freeze well and may be stored, frozen, for up to 4 months. Alternatively, prepare these dishes a day in advance. Chill the cooled soup, covered and re-heat over moderate heat, stirring, until just below simmering. Get ahead and crumble topping over fruit and chill, covered. Cook from chilled whilst you are eating main course.

SIMPLE TIME PLAN
To eat at: **1.20pm** and assuming that you are going to prepare the entire meal, from scratch. However, I strongly recommend that you read the introduction and prepare at least one item in advance.

11.40am	Prepare and cook soup. Leave to simmer. If including, prepare and cook pears. Set aside.
12.00pm	Prepare and dress the coleslaw. Chill covered in fridge.
12.05pm	Cook the new potatoes.
12.15pm	Check potatoes and turn heat off. Leave potatoes in their water covered, until service.
12.25am	Whiz soup in the food processor. Return to pan.
12.50pm	Marinate tuna fish. Prepare Feta salad, if using. Chill, with prepared dressing, in a separate jug.
1.00pm	Pre-heat oven to 180C (160 fan), Gas 4. Warm bread and cook stuffed mushrooms if including, in the oven, for 10-15 minutes.
1.10pm	Cook tuna.
1.15pm	Pop crumble into oven to cook. Set timer for 30 minutes. Re-heat soup.
1.20pm	Dress feta salad.

BUTTERNUT SQUASH AND ONION SOUP

1 tablespoon olive oil
25g butter
1 large onion, peeled and chopped
1 celery stalk, chopped
1 large butternut squash, (approx 1 Kg), peeled, de-seeded and chopped
2 level teaspoons medium hot curry powder
1 litre chicken or vegetable stock
400ml coconut milk

To serve: freshly chopped coriander, bread rolls or walnut bread, sliced

Put oil and butter into a large saucepan and heat until foaming. Add onion, celery and squash. Stir well. Cover and cook over medium heat, for 10 minutes, stirring once.

Add curry powder and continue to cook, stirring for 1 minute. Add stock and bring to the boil. Cover and simmer for 25 minutes, until squash is tender.
Blend until smooth in food processor, using metal blade, in which case you may need to blend soup in two batches or, alternatively, blend with a hand held wand type blender.

Add coconut milk and re-heat, stirring for 5 minutes.

Divide between warmed bowls and serve immediately sprinkled with coriander. Accompany soup with warmed bread.

MARINATED TUNA

6 tuna steaks, about 150g each
Juice 1 lemon
Approx 3 teaspoons blackened Cajun seasoning
2 tablespoons olive oil

Lay tuna in a shallow dish, in a single layer. Sprinkle with lemon juice and coat both sides of fish with Cajun seasoning.

Set aside for 15 minutes, or cover and chill for up to 3 hours.

When ready to cook, heat a griddle pan or frying pan. Lightly oil tuna steaks, on both sides. Cook steaks for 1-2 minutes on each side. You may have to do this in batches.

Keep tuna warm until ready to serve.

RED & GREEN COLESLAW

As an alternative, add 1 teaspoon medium hot curry powder to the dressing.

1 small white pointed cabbage
Half a red cabbage
4 spring onions
2 large carrots, peeled
1 large Cox's apple
5 ready to eat dried apricots, chopped

For the dressing
Grated rind & juice 1 medium orange
3 tablespoons mayonnaise
3 tablespoons crème fraiche
Salt & black pepper

Using a chopping board and a large chef's knife, finely shred cabbage, discarding central cores.

Turn into a large serving bowl.

Wash and finely chop spring onions. Add to bowl.

Grate carrots and add to bowl.

Core and chop unpeeled apple roughly. Add to bowl, with the apricots.

Prepare dressing. In a small bowl, combine rind and juice of orange, mayonnaise, crème fraiche and a seasoning of salt and pepper. Stir to blend. Taste and adjust seasoning, if necessary.

Pour dressing over coleslaw ingredients. Toss well, serve.

Extra Vegetable Dish
Stuffed Mushrooms

Clean and remove stalks from 12 medium size button mushrooms.

Brush mushrooms, all over with a little olive oil. Arrange, in a single layer, in a shallow roasting dish.

Transfer a 250g carton cream cheese with garlic and herbs to a mixing bowl.

Chop mushroom stalks finely and stir into cream cheese. Add a seasoning of salt and pepper. Stuff each mushroom with some of the cheese mixture. Return to roasting dish.

Bake in an oven pre-heated to 180C (160 fan), Gas 4, for 15 minutes, or so, while you are warming the bread.

PLUM AND BLACKBERRRY CRUMBLE WITH BRAZIL NUTS

Easy: Ready in 1 hour approx

750g ripe plums, Victoria's if possible, halved and stoned, then quartered
250g blackberries
100g caster sugar
1 teaspoon ground cinnamon

For the crumble
100g plain flour
125g seed and grain bread flour or wholemeal flour
100g chilled, unsalted butter, diced
75g caster sugar
50g Brazil nuts (optional) chopped
To Serve: Custard, cream or vanilla ice cream

Pre heat oven to 180C (160 fan), Gas 4.

Start by making the crumble. Put the flour and butter into a mixing bowl and rub butter into flour, using finger tips, until mixture resembles fine breadcrumbs. Alternatively, whiz in a food processor, using the metal blade, until mixture resembles breadcrumbs. Stir in sugar and Brazil nuts, if using.

In a fairly shallow dish approx. 26cm x 26cm, mix plums and blackberries. Sprinkle with caster sugar and cinnamon.
Spoon the crumble thickly over fruit to cover completely.

Stand on baking sheet and bake in centre of oven for 35-40 minutes until golden. Serve warm with custard, cream or ice cream.

Extra Dessert
Poached Pears in Fruity Tea

Put 50g Demerara sugar into a large saucepan with 1 tablespoon runny honey, 1 tablespoon redcurrant jelly, and 2 fresh and fruity cranberry, raspberry and elderflower tea bags.

Add 1 cinnamon stick. Carefully, pour over 600ml boiling water. Stir to dissolve sugar. Add 6 peeled, quartered and cored ripe, but firm pears. Cover and simmer for 10-15 minutes, until pears are just tender.

Transfer pears to serving dish, using a slotted spoon. Boil liquid fast, for a few minutes, until syrupy. Discard cinnamon stick and tea bags. Add about 6 sprigs redcurrants to the pears.

Pour over the warm syrup and serve with a spoonful of yoghurt or crème fraiche.

Menu 11

MENU 4
New Year's Eve Supper

Serves 6
Some skill needed: Ready in 2 hours, if casserole has been frozen and de-frosted

* Parma Ham with Fresh Pear & Dolcellata Salad
* Hungarian Goulash with Jacket Potatoes
* Dressed Mixed Salad
* Eton Mess

COOK'S HINTS AND TIPS

The casserole can be slowly cooked, up to two months in advance and frozen. Alternatively, cook a day in advance and hold chilled. Re-heat in pre-heated moderate oven for approximately one hour.

Both the pudding and starter can be largely prepared during the morning and chilled until ready to serve.

New Year's Eve is the one day when most people, hopefully, are delighted to proffer offers of help. Accept gratefully and ask one couple to bring the starter, another, the dessert!

You could always e-mail recipes to them. This simple bit of forward planning will allow you time to concentrate on the main course and house preparations.

As it is New Year's Eve, why not serve mulled wine, using the recipe on page 5? I usually make the mulled wine during the afternoon, then re-heat it gently, to serve as guests start to arrive. You may also like to hand round a platter of nibbles. Try whole sweet mini peppers, drained well and filled with goat's cheese. Celery boats filled with peanut butter and/or cream cheese are always popular as are tiny triangles of wholemeal bread, buttered and topped with smoked salmon, sprinkled with a little lemon juice and served with black pepper.

SIMPLE TIME PLAN

To eat at: **8pm**
Assuming the casserole was frozen and is now in the fridge, de-frosting.

6.00pm	Wash salad leaves. Dry in salad spinner or clean tea towel. Bag up in plastic bag, seal and chill until ready to use.
6.15pm	Prepare salad dressing. Chill.
6.25pm	Prepare Eton Mess up to the point where cream, fruit and meringue are combined. Cover mixing bowl with cling film and chill in the fridge until ready to serve, then quickly combine after eating main course.
6.30pm	Pre-heat oven to 200C (180 fan), Gas 6. Take goulash out of fridge.
6.35pm	Mark each jacket potato with a cross. Brush with a little olive oil and sprinkle with salt. Stand on baking sheet and place in top of oven.

7.00pm	Reduce oven temperature to 180C (160 fan), Gas 4-5. Put goulash casserole into oven to re-heat. This will take approx. 1 hour.
7.15pm	Toast pine nuts for starter. Set aside.
7.25pm	Prepare salad for starter. Arrange on side plates. Cover and chill.
7.35pm	Complete starters.
7.50pm	Check goulash and stir. Return to oven for about 15 minutes until piping hot. Complete mixed salad. Dress main course salad as you serve it. Put some soured cream and butter onto the table for the jacket potatoes.
8.00pm	Sit down to eat starter.

PARMA HAM WITH FRESH PEAR & DOLCELLATA SALAD

You could use chopped roasted peanuts in place of the pine nuts.

2 ripe pears, halved, cored and sliced
Juice ½ lemon, strained
1 tablespoon fresh thyme leaves
Salt & black pepper
1 bunch watercress, washed and dried
1-2 heads pink chicory, washed and dried
100g Parma ham
75g Dolcelatta cheese, diced
25g pine nut kernels, optional
1-2 tablespoons sesame oil
To serve: sliced chunks of wholemeal bread

Brush pear slices with lemon juice. Sprinkle with thyme and season with salt and pepper.

Combine watercress and chicory. Divide between 6 side plates.

Toast pine nuts, briefly in a non-stick frying pan until lightly golden.
Arrange ham and pears on each plate, to side of salad.
Top with a little diced cheese and sprinkle with pine nuts, if using.
Serve, drizzling sesame oil, over salad. Accompany salad with a basket of bread.

HUNGARIAN GOULASH

Note: To prepare peppers quickly: hold each pepper on chopping board, stalk uppermost, remove "cheeks" of each pepper and you will be left with stalk and seeds which you discard. Dice peppers.
A little effort needed: Ready in 3 hours

900g stewing beef or chuck steak, trimmed and cut into 2.5cm dice
3 tablespoons olive oil
2 large red onions, roughly chopped
2 cloves garlic, crushed
1 rounded tablespoon plain flour
2 rounded tablespoons Hungarian smoked paprika
Salt and black pepper
3 tablespoons tomato purée
1 tablespoon Worcestershire sauce
2 x 400g cans chopped tomatoes
150ml beef stock
1 medium red pepper, de-seeded and chopped
1 medium yellow pepper, de-seeded and chopped
150ml soured cream, optional but nice
To serve: large handful freshly chopped parsley or 2 tablespoons chopped chives

Pre-heat oven to 140C (120 fan), Gas 1.

Heat the oil in a large frying pan and brown the cubes of beef all over. You will need to do this in batches. Transfer browned beef to a plate, lined with kitchen paper.

Add onions to pan and cook over medium heat, for about 8 minutes, stirring occasionally. The onions should be softened and golden. Add crushed garlic and continue to cook for 1 minute.

Sprinkle in flour and paprika and stir to soak up juices. Stir in tomato purée and Worcestershire sauce.

Put beef and onion mixture into a large casserole dish. Add the tins of tomatoes and the stock. Season with salt, and pepper. Bring to simmering point. Cover with a lid, transfer to oven and cook for 2½ hours.

Stir in chopped peppers, replace lid and continue to cook for a further 30 minutes, until meat is meltingly tender. Check seasoning, adding a little more, if necessary.

When ready to serve, stir soured cream into casserole, if using, and serve sprinkled with parsley or chives.

DRESSED MIXED SALAD WITH DIJON MUSTARD DRESSING

1 Cos (Romaine) lettuce, washed and dried
2 large handfuls rocket
4 spring onions, sliced
1 bunch watercress, washed and dried, discarding any tough stems
1 red pepper, de-seeded and thinly sliced

For the dressing
5 tablespoons extra virgin olive oil
2 heaped tablespoons Dijon mustard
2 tablespoons white wine vinegar
Salt & freshly ground black pepper

Tear lettuce leaves into ribbons and put into a large salad bowl with rocket, spring onions, watercress, and red pepper.

Prepare dressing. Put all ingredients for dressing into a screw top jar. Cover tightly with a lid. Shake well. Taste and adjust seasoning.

When ready to eat, pour dressing over salad ingredients. Toss together and serve.

ETON MESS

Should you prefer to use more seasonal fruits, use 2 mangoes with 2 x 225g punnets of blackberries. Mangos, although imported are very good around Christmas time.

1 x 225g punnet raspberries
2 x 225g punnets strawberries
Sieved icing sugar, to taste
600ml (1 pint) double cream, whipped
6 meringue nests bought from the supermarket, broken into fairly large pieces
6 scoops good quality vanilla ice cream (I like Carte d'Or)
6 raspberries to decorate

In a large mixing bowl, roughly crush together raspberries and strawberries. Stir in icing sugar to taste.

In a separate large mixing bowl, whip cream until it holds its shape. Lightly fold crushed fruit into cream.

Fold in meringue pieces.

To serve, place a scoop of vanilla ice cream into each of 6 chilled sundae dishes. Top evenly with fool mixture. Serve immediately, decorating each dessert with a raspberry.

MENU 5
Speedy Light Lunch

Serves 6
A little effort needed: Ready in 1 hour approx.

Salmon fillets can be a bit pricy, but as salmon is an oily fish, it is fairly filling, so small fillets are fine. Hopefully you followed the advice in Credit Crunch Know How at the beginning of this book, and have fillets of salmon in the freezer!

* Sesame Salmon with Crème Fraiche Sauce, Roast Tomatoes & Noodles of your choice
* Salad with Feta Cheese
* Strawberries Dipped in Chocolate

The pink salmon looks really appetising, alongside the brightly coloured roast tomatoes. Both have wonderful flavours.

COOKS HINTS & TIPS

Prepare strawberries duing the morning.

Cook noodles at the last minute.

To toast sesame seeds: Place seeds in a non-stick frying pan with 1 teaspoon corn oil. Cook over medium heat, tossing pan regularly, for approximately one minute, until seeds are lightly golden.

SIMPLE TIME PLAN

To eat at: **1pm,**

12.30pm	Prepare salmon then set aside. Pre-heat oven to 200C (180 fan), Gas 7.
12.40pm	Cook tomatoes, towards top of oven.
12.40pm	Prepare salad ingredients and chill in a bowl. Prepare dressing and chill in a screw top jar.
12.45pm	Cook the salmon in centre of oven.
12.50pm	Prepare crème fraiche sauce for salmon. Put kettle on for noodles.
12.55pm	Pour boiling water onto noodles.
1pm	Serve.

SESAME SALMON WITH CRÈME FRAICHE SAUCE & ROAST TOMATOES

12 medium sized tomatoes, on the vine
1 tablespoon olive oil
6 x 125g salmon fillets, skinned
Salt and black pepper
1½ tablespoons lightly toasted sesame seeds
225g noodles of choice
2 teaspoons toasted sesame oil
1 tablespoon freshly chopped coriander
To serve: wedges of lime or lemon

Pre-heat oven to 200C (180 fan), Gas 6.

Put tomatoes, still on vine into a roasting tin. Brush with the olive oil.
Roast towards top of oven for 20 minutes.
Meanwhile, put the salmon onto a non-stick baking sheet. Brush with a little oil. Season with salt, and pepper. Sprinkle with toasted sesame seeds.

Cook salmon, below tomatoes for approximately 12-15 minutes, until fish flakes when pushed with point of a knife.

Cook noodles, according to directions on pack. Drain well and turn into warmed serving dish.

Toss with sesame oil and coriander. Serve garnished with lime or lemon wedges.

CRÈME FRAICHE SAUCE

8 rounded tablespoons crème fraiche, low fat, if preferred
2 rounded tablespoons mayonnaise, reduced fat, if preferred
1 teaspoon lemon juice
2 level teaspoons tomato ketchup
Salt and pepper

In a medium bowl, combine all ingredients. Check seasoning, adding a little more, if necessary.

Serve separately to accompany fish.

SALAD WITH FETA CHEESE

4 little Gem lettuces, divided into leaves, washed and drained
2 handfuls rocket, washed and drained
1 marinated red pepper, sliced
8 pimento stuffed olives, halved, optional
100g Feta cheese, cubed

For the dressing
3 tablespoons olive oil
1 clove garlic, crushed
1 teaspoon Dijon mustard
Grated rind and strained juice ½ lemon
Salt and black pepper
½ red chilli, chopped

Put all ingredients for salad into a large salad bowl.
Prepare dressing. Put all ingredients for dressing into a bowl.
Whisk to combine. Check seasoning, adding a little more, if necessary.
When ready to serve, pour dressing over leaves. Toss to coat, serve immediately.

STRAWBERRIES DIPPED IN CHOCOLATE

These strawberries can be prepared during the morning to eat at supper time but will not keep much longer than this.

450g strawberries, approximately
350g white chocolate
350g dark chocolate

Or

350g milk chocolate

Prepare 2 baking trays, by covering them with parchment or waxed paper.

In two large, separate mixing bowls, melt each type of chocolate over pans of hot water, stirring frequently. Ensure bowls do not touch water.

Stir chocolate until smooth.

Wipe strawberries clean leaving stalks intact. Dip half strawberries in white chocolate, and remaining strawberries in dark or milk chocolate, to coat ½ of each fruit.

Carefully place on prepared trays.

Chill to set – this only takes about 5-10 minutes.

Transfer to a pretty plate and serve at room temperature.

MENU 6
Supper for Friends
Serves 6
Easy: Ready in 1 hour 5 minutes approx.

* Carrot & Parsnip Soup
* Spicy Shepherd's Pie
* Roast Carrots & Courgettes
* Melon, Mango & Stem Ginger Fruit Salad

COOK'S HINTS & TIPS

The soup freezes well, so could be made well in advance. Freeze without the milk, which you stir in to the de-frosted soup, before re-heating.

Should you wish to "get ahead" you could make the shepherds pie early on and bake it when guests arrive.

Chill the prepared pie, without grilling, until 45 minutes before serving.

Re-heat in oven pre-heated to 190C (170 fan), Gas 5 for approximately 45 minutes, until golden. There will be no need to grill the potato in this case.

SIMPLE TIME PLAN

To eat at: **8.15pm**

6.55pm	Pre-heat oven to 180C (160 fan), Gas 4.
7.00pm	Prepare vegetables for roasting and soup.
7.10pm	Roast vegetables toward top of oven. Prepare and cook soup.
7.15pm	Whilst vegetables for soup are cooking, prepare shepherd's pie.
	Prepare mince first. Whilst filling is cooking, prepare and cook potatoes.
7.40pm	In a food processor, whiz soup. Return to pan. Add milk and set aside.
7.50pm	Increase oven temperature to 200C (180 fan), Gas 7. Stir vegetables and return to oven. Pre-heat the grill to hot. Prepare topping for shepherd's pie.
8.00pm	Put shepherd's pie under grill until golden.
	In oven, warm bread, for 10 minutes, below the vegetables. Re-heat soup gently, stirring. Switch oven off. Keep shepherd's pie warm in switched off oven. Prepare fruit salad.
8.15pm	Serve soup. Remove fruit salad from fridge and leave to stand at room temperature until ready to serve.

CARROT & PARSNIP SOUP

50g butter
450g carrots, peeled and sliced
3 large parsnips, peeled and sliced
1 medium leek, trimmed, washed and sliced
2 small potatoes, peeled and chopped
1 level tablespoon freshly grated root ginger
Grated rind ½ small orange
1 bunch coriander, chopped
1 litre hot vegetable stock
100ml semi-skimmed milk
Salt and black pepper
2 teaspoons runny honey

To serve: ciabatta bread, warmed in oven for 10 minutes or so.

In a large saucepan melt butter. Add carrots, parsnips, leek and potatoes. Sauté for 8-10 minutes.

Add ginger, orange rind, coriander and stock. Bring to the boil. Simmer covered, for 25 minutes.

Whiz soup in a blender, using metal blade, in which case you may need to whiz in 2 batches, or use a hand held, wand type blender.

Return soup to clean pan. Add milk. Re-heat to serve, stirring occasionally.

Check seasoning, adding salt and pepper if necessary. Stir in honey. Serve, with the warmed bread.

SPICY SHEPHERD'S PIE

If you don't have a large frying pan with a lid, use tin foil and make a cover.

2 tablespoons sunflower or corn oil
700g raw, lean minced lamb
1 medium onion, chopped
1 celery stick, finely chopped
1 carrot, peeled and chopped
1 clove garlic, chopped
1 tablespoon fresh root ginger, peeled and grated
1½ teaspoons garam masala
½ teaspoon truly lazy chillies, or 1 red chilli, de-seeded and chopped
1 tablespoon tomato purée
1 rounded tablespoon plain flour
600ml hot lamb or chicken stock
Salt
750g floury potatoes, such as Désirée, cut into large, even sized chunks
50g butter
3 tablespoons milk
1 bunch spring onions, sliced

Heat 1 tablespoon of the oil in a large frying pan.

Brown minced lamb, over fairly high heat, in two batches. Remove with a slotted spoon and set aside.

Add remaining oil and fry onion, celery and carrot for 10 minutes, until softened. Pour off excess fat.

Add garlic, garam masala and chilli and cook for 1 minute. Stir in flour and tomato purée. Cook for 2 minutes.

Gradually stir in the hot stock.

Return the mince to the pan. Season, with a little salt. Bring to boil, simmer gently, covered, for 30 minutes.

Meanwhile, cook potatoes in a pan of lightly-salted, boiling water for 15-20 minutes, until tender. Drain well. Pre-heat grill to hot.

Mash potatoes with butter and milk. Fold in spring onions.

Tip lamb mixture into an oven proof dish.

Top with mashed potato. Grill until golden and serve with the roast vegetables.

ROAST CARROTS & COURGETTES

6 large carrots, peeled and sliced
8 courgettes, topped, tailed and sliced
3 tablespoons olive oil
2 tablespoons freshly chopped parsley
2 cloves garlic, crushed
Salt and black pepper

Pre-heat oven to 200C (180C fan), Gas 6.

Put prepared carrots into large roasting tin. Add courgettes and oil.

Toss using two spoons. Season, with salt, and pepper. Add parsley and garlic. Toss again.

Roast near top of oven for approx. 45 minutes until tender and tinged golden.

Serve immediately.

MELON, MANGO & STEM GINGER SALAD

1 large ripe Galia melon
2 mangoes
1 level dessert spoon sieved icing sugar, optional
1 piece from a jar of stem ginger in syrup, optional
100ml orange or apple juice, from a carton
To serve: ½ fat crème fraiche, chocolate biscuits, optional

Cut melon in half and discard seeds.

Remove melon flesh from skin in one of two ways: You can either cut each melon half, into slices, and dice the flesh or alternatively use a melon baller and scoop out "balls" of melon.

Put prepared melon into a large serving bowl.

Peel mangoes, cut flesh from central stones and dice. Add to bowl. Sprinkle over icing sugar, if using.

Chop stem ginger into fine dice, if using, and add to bowl. Pour over orange or apple juice. Toss gently to mix.

Serve or cover and chill until ready to serve, accompanied by the chocolate biscuits, if using.

MENU 7
Easter Sunday Lunch
Serves 6
A little effort needed: Ready in 2 hours approx.

* Herbed Roast Shoulder of Lamb
* Roasted New Potatoes with Salsa
* Mange-tout & Carrots with Sage & Lemon Butter
* Baked White Chocolate Cheesecake with Strawberries

There is no need to serve a starter for this menu, but perhaps offer some slices of ripe melon, and a selection of olives, for guests to hand round while you put the finishing touches to the roast.

COOK'S HINTS & TIPS
Ask the butcher to bone and roll the lamb for you, but not to tie it, as you are adding a stuffing. Whatever you do, don't use plastic string to tie the lamb!
The cheesecake is easy to make and delicious. It can be made well in advance and frozen for up to 2 months. De-frost over night, in fridge.
Serve the roasted new potatoes with or without the salsa.
You may like to serve the red wine gravy from Menu 1 with the lamb.
The cooked lamb will hold heat for at least 20 minutes, once removed from oven. The flavour and texture of meat improves on standing.

SIMPLE TIME PLAN
Assuming cheesecake is frozen.
To eat at: **1.35pm**

09.00am	Remove cheesecake from freezer and transfer to fridge until 1pm.
11.10am	Pre-heat oven to 190C (170 fan), Gas 5,
11.15am	Scrub potatoes and place in bowl. Add remaining ingredients for roasting.
11.20am	Prepare carrots and mange-tout. Set aside.
11.30am	Put lamb into oven.
11.35am	Lay table, prepare strawberries and decorate cheesecake.
1.00pm	Put potatoes into oven, above lamb.
1.10pm	Remove lamb and allow to rest, covered with a tent of foil. Increase oven temperature to 200C, 400F, Gas 6.
1.15pm	Cook carrots and mange-tout. Prepare salsa for potatoes.
1.20pm	Carve lamb.
1.30pm	Transfer carrots and mange-tout to a warmed vegetable dish. Cover and keep warm.
1.35pm	Checking potatoes are tender, spoon salsa over and serve.

HERBED ROAST SHOULDER OF LAMB

1 x 2.5kg shoulder of lamb, boned

For the Stuffing:
50g fresh wholemeal breadcrumbs
1 red onion, peeled and finely chopped
1 tablespoon freshly chopped parsley
1 tablespoon chopped mint
½ whole nutmeg, grated
Grated rind ½ lemon
1 large egg, beaten
Salt and black pepper
4 sprigs rosemary
To Serve: Redcurrant jelly

Pre-heat oven to 190C (170 fan), Gas 5.

Prepare stuffing: In a mixing bowl, combine the breadcrumbs, onion, parsley, and mint.

Add nutmeg and lemon rind. Season well with salt and pepper. Stir in beaten egg, to bind mixture.

Unroll lamb and spread stuffing evenly over.

Roll the lamb up as neatly as possible and tie with string, to secure, at various places, along length of joint.

Place rosemary sprigs in roasting tin, then place lamb on top.

Roast in pre-heated oven, allowing 25 minutes per 450g.

Once cooked, remove lamb from tin and set aside to rest for 20 minutes, covered with a tent of foil, before removing string and carving. Use juices from pan to spoon over lamb on serving, just pour off excess fat beforehand.

Extra veg.

You may like to add this simple vegetable dish which cooks while the lamb is resting.

Halve 5 medium tomatoes, horizontally and place, cut side up in a lightly-oiled roasting tin. Brush with a little olive oil, season well with salt and pepper. Sprinkle with a handful of freshly chopped thyme and basil leaves. Roast in the oven for 20 minutes.

ROASTED NEW POTATOES WITH SALSA

750g new potatoes, scrubbed clean and halved, if large
1 teaspoon freshly ground sea salt
3 teaspoons coriander seeds, lightly crushed
2 garlic cloves, peeled and chopped
3 tablespoons olive oil
6 tablespoons canned, chopped tomatoes
4 ripe fresh tomatoes cut into thin wedges
4 tablespoons freshly chopped coriander leaves
Salt and black pepper

Preheat oven to 200C (180 fan), Gas 6.
Put the potatoes into a large roasting tin. In a mixing bowl, combine sea salt. coriander seeds, garlic and olive oil. Add to the potatoes. Toss to coat.
Roast for 25-30 minutes, until softened and golden.
In a small bowl combine the remaining ingredients. Season, with salt, and pepper.
Spoon salsa over the hot potatoes and serve immediately.

MANGE-TOUT & CARROTS WITH SAGE & LEMON BUTTER

750g young carrots, scraped clean and trimmed
25g butter
1 teaspoon caster sugar
400g mange-tout, washed
1 tablespoon whole small sage leaves
Juice 1 lemon
Salt & freshly ground black pepper

Bring a large pan of lightly-salted water to the boil. Add carrots and simmer covered, for approximately 5 minutes.
Drain and steam dry in colander for 2-3 minutes.
Melt butter in a wok or large frying pan with the sugar.
Add drained carrots with the mange-tout and sage. Heat stirring, over a medium heat, for 1-2 minutes, until carrots are lightly golden.
Add lemon juice and a seasoning of salt and pepper.
Serve immediately.

WHITE CHOCOLATE CHEESECAKE WITH STRAWBERRIES

125g dark chocolate digestive biscuits
150g digestive biscuits
125g butter
400g white chocolate
400g light cream cheese
3 large eggs
To decorate
8 strawberries, halved
To decorate: 8 strawberries, halved
To Serve: Single cream

You will need 1x 22cm loose bottomed or spring formed cake tin, lightly greased with a little of the butter.
Pre-heat oven to 170C (150 fan), Gas 3.
Crush biscuits into crumbs, using a food processor fitted with a metal blade, or in a large plastic bag, using a rolling pin to bash biscuits into crumbs.
Melt butter in a large saucepan. Remove from heat and add biscuits crumbs.
Mix well.
Turn into prepared cake tin and press down with back of a metal spoon to form cheesecake base.
Chill in fridge.
Stirring frequently, melt chocolate in a mixing bowl over a pan of simmering water. Do not allow bowl to touch water.
Once melted, remove bowl from pan and set aside for 5 minutes to allow chocolate to cool slightly.
In a large mixing bowl, gradually add melted chocolate, to cream cheese, beating it in with a wooden spoon. Beat in eggs one at a time. Continue to beat until smooth.
Pour mixture into cake tin.
Stand tin on a baking sheet and bake in centre of oven for 45-50 minutes until cheesecake is just set but still has a bit of a wobble.
Remove from oven and set aside to cool completely.
Wrap and freeze at this point.
Serve the cheesecake decorated with the strawberries, accompanied by single cream.

MENU 8
Delicious Weekend Menu

Serves 6
Some skill required: Ready in 1½ hours approx.

* Fish Pie with Salmon, Prawns & Dill
* Cauliflower and Broccoli
* Decadent Chocolate Cake

Pollock is a cheaper, eco-friendly alternative to cod. Don't be scared to use it in this recipe as it tastes delicious. Coley is another well-flavoured, low-cost fish that is completely overlooked. It makes an excellent fish pie.

Buy a whole cauliflower and 1 head broccoli.

N.B Prepare and cook the chocolate cake a day in advance, but do not fill or ice it. When cold, store in an airtight tin.

COOK'S HINTS & TIPS

Everyone loves a really good fish pie. This one can be prepared in the morning, chilled until ready to bake. Tasty and sustaining, an excellent lunch or supper dish.

Ask the fishmonger to skin and fillet the fish for you.

You may also like to also serve frozen peas with the fish pie. In which case, cook according to directions on packet.

SIMPLE TIME PLAN

Assuming cake has been made.
To eat at: **7pm**

5.25pm	Peel and cook the potatoes.
5.35pm	Prepare sauce for the pie.
5.50pm	Assemble fish pie. Break cauliflower and broccoli into florettes and place in saucepan.
6.00pm	Pre-heat oven to 200C (180 fan), Gas 6.
6.10pm	Bake fish pie.
6.15pm	Prepare ganache and use to ice cake.
6.50pm	Simmer cauliflower and broccoli florettes in chicken or vegetable stock, for 7-8 minutes, until tender. Drain well and serve with melted butter.
7.00pm	Serve.

FISH PIE WITH SALMON & DILL

A delicious mixture of oily and white fish with a cheese topping makes this pie very special.

You will need 6 individual pie dishes about 300ml capacity or, if preferred, one large pie dish.

Topping
1kg floury white potatoes such as King Edward or Maris Piper, peeled
25g butter
4 tablespoons whole milk
75g Cheddar cheese, grated, optional
Salt & freshly ground black pepper

Filling
50g butter
4 tablespoons plain flour
400ml whole milk
2 tablespoons fresh dill, chopped
450g salmon, skinned and filleted
450g white fish such as coley, pollock, cod or haddock, skinned and filleted
100g raw large prawns, peeled, optional but nice

Cut potatoes into chunks and put into a saucepan. Cover with cold water and add about ½ teaspoon salt. Cover pan with a lid. Bring to boil, simmer for approx. 20 minutes until tender.

Drain immediately, mash well with butter, milk and grated cheese, if using. Add a little seasoning. Beat well with a wooden spoon until smooth and creamy. Whilst potatoes are cooking, prepare filling.

Cut fish into chunks and set aside on a dinner plate. Halve prawns.

Make white sauce. Melt butter in a medium saucepan. Stir in flour until grainy. Gradually add milk, stirring continuously, over medium heat, to make a smooth white sauce. If lumps appear, beat vigorously with a balloon whisk.

Fold in chopped dill. Season, with salt and pepper. Gently fold in fish.

Turn into pie dish or dishes and set aside to cool slightly.
Pre-heat oven to 200C (180 fan), Gas 6.

Spoon mashed potato over fish mixture. Spread out to cover.

Mark potato into a lattice pattern using a fork.

Put pie or pies onto a baking sheet and bake small pies for approx. 25 minutes or the large pie for approx. 35 minutes until golden.

DECADENT CHOCOLATE CAKE

Short of time? Use a 450g pot Betty Crocker Ready to Spread Icing as filling and icing instead of the ganache.

225g butter or margarine softened, plus extra for greasing
225g caster sugar
4 large eggs, beaten
200g self raising flour
2 tablespoons cocoa powder
1 teaspoon baking powder
2 tablespoons milk
3 tablespoons chocolate spread
150ml double or whipping cream

For the ganache
175g Green & Blacks plain cooking chocolate, broken into pieces
75g butter, softened
4 tablespoons double cream
To Decorate: a few fresh strawberries, optional
Your will need 2 x 20cm sandwich tins, greased and lined

Pre-heat oven to 180C (160 fan), Gas 4.

Make the cake by one stage method. Put butter, sugar, and eggs into a large mixing bowl. Add sifted flour, cocoa powder and baking powder. Add milk.

Using electric beaters, on low speed, beat until combined.

Increase speed and continue to beat for 1 minute, until light and creamy.

Divide evenly between prepared tins. Level surface and bake for 25-30 minutes, until cooked, well risen, and springy to the touch.

Turn out and cool completely, on wire rack.

Spread chocolate spread onto 1 cake. Whip cream until stiff, spread over chocolate spread. Top with remaining cake.

For the ganache:
Melt chocolate, butter and cream in a bowl over a pan of simmering water.

Stir once until smooth.

Arrange filled cake on serving plate.

Pour ganache over centre of cake, spread with a knife to let icing run down sides evenly. Decorate with strawberries, if using.

MENU 9
Family Supper
Serves 6
Straight Forward: Ready in 1 hour approx.

* Chilli Con Carne with Garlic Bread
* Easy Apple Tarts with Ice Cream
* Chocolate Mousse.

You might like to include, Easy guacamole from Menu 16, and perhaps select a salad from one of the other menus, to serve with the chilli.

Garlic bread is very popular; however rice or pita bread could be served as an alternative.

To make your own garlic bread: Buy 3 half size French sticks and make slashes along length of each, but do not cut right through. Beat 3 crushed garlic cloves into 100g softened butter with a handful freshly chopped parsley. Using a knife push a little of the butter into each opening. Wrap each loaf, separately in foil to make a loosely sealed parcel. Stand loaves in a roasting tin and bake in a pre-heated oven, 190C (170 fan), Gas 5 for approximately 15 minutes.

COOK'S HINTS & TIPS

Prepare guacamole, if including, just before serving as it tends to discolour quickly. Select lean British minced beef for the chilli.

If including the extra dessert, aim to get ahead and make the chocolate mousse in the morning, or the day before. Store chilled.

The apple tarts are simplicity itself to prepare and cook, but taste so delicious that people will think you spent hours over a hot stove preparing them!

SIMPLE TIME PLAN

To eat at: **8pm**

6.20pm	Make chilli con carne. Keep warm, once cooked.
6.40pm	Pre-heat oven to 220C (fan 200) Gas 7. Prepare apple tarts.
7.00pm	Cook apple tarts.
7.25 pm	Reduce oven temperature to 190C, 170 fan , Gas 5. Put garlic bread into oven.
7.40pm	Prepare salad, if required.
7.50pm	Prepare guacamole.
8.00pm	Serve.

CHILLI CON CARNE

1 tablespoon olive oil
1 large onion, finely chopped
1 fat clove garlic, crushed
2 large red chillis, de-seeded and chopped or 1½ teaspoons chilli powder
700g lean minced beef
125g bacon lardons
1 red pepper, de-seeded and chopped
2 x 400g cans chopped tomatoes
125ml beef stock
2 tablespoons tomato purée
Salt and black pepper
2 x 400g cans red kidney beans, rinsed and drained
To serve: garlic bread, freshly chopped parsley.

Make chilli. In a large saucepan, heat oil.
Add onion and chillis. Fry for approximately 5 minutes, until soft and golden.
Add beef and bacon. Continue to fry, stirring, for 7-8 minutes until browned.

Pour off excess fat, as it appears, to aid browning.

Stir in garlic and continue to cook, stirring for 1 minute.
Stir in red pepper, tomatoes, beef stock, tomato purée and a little salt and pepper.

Bring to the boil, cover and simmer gently, for 20 minutes.
Add kidney beans and continue to simmer for 15 minutes.

Towards end of cooking, heat garlic bread in pre-heated oven according to pack instructions, or make your own. See introduction to this menu.

Serve chilli, sprinkled with the chopped parsley and accompanied by the garlic bread.

EASY APPLE TARTS

Makes 7 tarts

**1x 500g block puff pastry, de-frosted, if frozen
1 large Bramley apple
2 eating apples, Cox's if possible
2 tablespoons lemon juice
50g butter, melted
4 teaspoons Demerera sugar
1 teaspoon ground cinnamon
To Serve: Sifted icing sugar, vanilla ice cream**

Pre-heat oven to 220C (200 fan) Gas 7.

On a floured surface, roll pastry out to an oblong, approximately 38cm x 32cm.

Using a saucer as a guide, cut out 5 rounds of pastry. Re-roll pastry and cut out 2 more rounds. Divide pastry rounds between 2 baking sheets. Chill.

Peel, core and roughly chop apples. Put into a mixing bowl, and toss in lemon juice to prevent browning.

Divide apple between pastry rounds, bringing it almost to edge of the pastry. Brush each tart with some of the melted butter. Combine cinnamon and Demerara sugar and sprinkle evenly over tarts.

Bake for approximately 20-25 minutes, until golden. Cool slightly.

Serve the tarts, dusted with a little icing sugar, accompanied by ice cream.

Extra dessert.
Chocolate mousse.

Break 200g plain or milk cooking chocolate, Green & Black's is good, into squares.

Put into a large mixing bowl, suspended over a pan of boiling water.
Melt chocolate, stirring frequently. Set aside.

Separate 5 large eggs, putting whites into a large clean mixing bowl.

Beat yolks, into chocolate, one at a time, using an electric mixer, until smooth.
If mixture goes "grainy" beat in a little hot water.

With clean whisks, beat egg whites until stiff. Fold into chocolate mixture using a metal spoon.

Divide between 6 ramekins and chill to set. Serve with a dollop of crème fraiche.

MENU 10
Classic Italian

Serves 6
Some skill needed: Ready in 2 hours approx.

* Mussels with Garlic & Cream
* Beef Lasagne
* Ciabatta Bread Salad
* Zabaglione

COOK'S HINTS & TIPS

Mussels are one of the "best" of British shellfish. Remember, shellfish is seasonal, so buy mussels only when there is an "r" in the month; from September to April.
You could use up any day old bread to make croutons for the salad.
Both the lasagne and Zabaglione can be prepared during the morning.

SIMPLE TIME PLAN

During the morning:

11.00am	Prepare lasagne, to point where it is sprinkled with grated cheese. Set aside to cool completely. When cold, chill in fridge until 30 minutes before baking.
12.00am	Prepare zabaglione. Chill in fridge.

To eat at 8pm

6.45pm	Soak Mussels.
7.00pm	Prepare salad. Chill in fridge in a sealed plastic bag or covered bowl. Remove lasagne from fridge. Pre-heat oven to 190C (170 fan), Gas 5.
7.15pm	Put prepared lasagne in oven to bake.
7.25pm	Lay table.
7.45pm	Prepare sauce for mussels.
7.47pm	Cook the mussels.
7.55pm	Check lasagne. Turn oven down. Dish up mussels and enjoy!
8.10pm	Serve lasagne and dressed salad.

MUSSELS WITH GARLIC AND CREAM

2Kg. mussels
120ml dry white wine
4 shallots, finely chopped
1 clove garlic, crushed
3 sprigs fresh thyme
100ml double cream
50g butter, cut into small dice
Salt and pepper
2 tablespoons freshly chopped parsley

Scrub mussels well and remove any beards, and barnacles from shells.
Discard any mussels that are open, or have broken shells
Put mussels into a large bowl.
Cover with cold water and leave to soak for at least 1 hour.

Put wine into a large stock pot and bring to the boil.
Add shallots, garlic and thyme. Add drained mussels.
Cover pan and cook for 5 minutes.
Shake pan or stir frequently until shells open.
Lift out mussels into a large soup tureen or bowl.
Discard any mussels that do not open.

Reduce cooking liquid by half by boiling and strain into a clean saucepan.
Add cream and bring to boil to thicken slightly.

Beat in the butter, a little at a time. Season to taste, with a little salt and pepper.
Add parsley and pour sauce over mussels to serve.

BEEF LASAGNE

1 tablespoon corn or vegetable oil
1 medium onion, chopped
1 medium carrot, chopped
700g lean minced beef
2 cloves garlic, crushed
1 x 400g can chopped tomatoes
2 tablespoons tomato purée
1 teaspoon dried coriander
125ml red wine, optional
200ml beef stock

For the white sauce
75g butter
75g butter
725ml whole milk, warmed
75 ml double cream
Salt and black pepper
Approx. 14 sheets ready to cook lasagne verde (with spinach)
50g cheddar cheese, grated
2 tablespoons grated parmesan cheese

You will need a lasagne dish approx. 32cm x 28cm a 6cm deep.

Prepare the meat sauce. Heat oil, in a large saucepan. Add onion and carrot. Cook stirring, over medium heat, until onion softens, approximately 5-7 minutes.

Add minced beef and continue to fry, until golden. Drain off excess fat, if necessary. Add garlic and continue to cook for 1 minute.

Add tomatoes with the coriander, tomato purée, red wine, if using and beef stock.

Season, with a little salt, and pepper.

Bring to the boil, stirring. Cover with a lid and simmer gently for 30 minutes. Set aside.

Prepare white sauce. Melt butter in a large non-stick saucepan.
Stir in flour and cook, stirring until a grainy roux results.
Remove from heat and stir in about one-third of the milk.
Return pan to heat and bring to boil, stirring continuously.
Repeat this process until all milk has been added and a smooth sauce results.
Simmer sauce for about 5 minutes, stirring occasionally. Set aside.

Assemble the lasagne. Pre-heat the oven to 190C (170 fan), Gas 5. Have beside you a large mixing bowl, full of hot water, from a boiled kettle.

Spoon one-third of the meat mixture over base of dish.

Cover meat sauce with some of the lasagne sheets, softening them briefly, in the hot water and shaking to drain first.

Beat cream into white sauce. Spread some of the white sauce over the lasagne. Continue to layer in this way until all ingredients have been used up, finishing with a layer of white sauce.

Combine grated cheddar and parmesan cheeses and sprinkle evenly over the top.
Bake in centre of oven for 30-40 minutes until top is golden.
Serve lasagne, cut into squares.

CIABATTA BREAD SALAD

250g ciabatta loaf, cut into 6-8 thick slices
2 tablespoons olive oil
4 large, ripe tomatoes chopped roughly
½ large cucumber halved, de-seeded and chopped
1 small iceberg lettuce, washed and dried, then sliced
1 medium red onion, finely sliced
Small handful fresh basil leaves

For the dressing
3 tablespoons red wine vinegar
6 tablespoons extra virgin olive oil
1 clove garlic, crushed
Salt and black pepper

Pre-heat oven to 200C (180 fan), Gas 6.

Prepare bread for salad. Cut or tear bread into chunks and place in a large mixing bowl.

Add olive oil and toss to coat bread with oil.
Turn onto 1 or 2 baking sheets.

Bake in hottest part of oven for 10-15 minutes until golden.
Remove from oven and set aside to cool completely.

Meanwhile, prepare salad dressing. Put all ingredients for the dressing into a screw top jar.

Shake well to combine. Taste and check seasoning. Set aside.

Prepare salad. Put tomatoes, cucumber, lettuce, onion and basil leaves into a large salad bowl. Add cooled ciabatta.

Shake dressing again. Pour over salad, toss together and serve immediately.

ZABAGLIONE

4 large egg yolks
4 tablespoons caster sugar
4 tablespoons Marsala wine, brandy or sweet sherry
Grated rind 1 lemon
To Serve: Lady Finger Biscuits, optional

Put egg yolks and sugar into a large, heat proof mixing bowl.
Place bowl over pan of gently simmering water.
Do not allow bowl to touch water.
Using an electric whisk, beat egg yolks and sugar, until thickened, to consistency, of whipped cream.

Add lemon rind. Gradually, beat in wine, drop by drop until fully combined and a light fluffy custard results.

Divide between 6 small wine glasses.

Allow to Cool. Chill until ready to serve.

MENU 11

Plan in Advance, Dinner Buffet Party

Serves 8-10
Skill needed: Ready in 2¼ hours approx.

* Baked Salmon with Dill
* Pork & Chorizo Stew with Olive Bread & Walnut Bread
* Spinach & Avocado Salad
* Lemon, Raspberry & Kiwi Fruit Pavlova

You may like to include mashed potatoes from menu 12.

Please note that the pork should marinade in the fridge for 24 hours before cooking, however if pressed for time, 2 hours will suffice.

This recipe for cooking salmon is ideal as it ensures a moist and perfectly cooked fish, every time. The salmon can be cooked up to a day in advance. Once cold, wrap loosely and chill in fridge.

Whole salmon is often sold at an amazingly good price. Use any leftovers the following day for a special salad.

You may need to cut the fish in half vertically to make it fit into your roasting tin. Arrange the two halves nose to tail on the sheet of foil.

COOK'S HINTS & TIPS

For better whipping, use egg whites at room temperature.

Use egg yolks from pavlova for a crème brulée or zabaglione. Egg yolks will keep for up to two days, covered, with cling film and chilled.

SIMPLE TIME PLAN

N.B. Prepare and cook pavlova base and salmon a day in advance.

To eat at: **7pm**

4.15pm	Prepare and cook pork stew.
5.30pm	Prepare salad and store in fridge. Make dressing and chill.
5.30pm	Prepare topping for pavlova. Decorate pavlova and chill in fridge.
6.00pm	Lay table.
6.40pm	Put bread in oven to warm.
6.45pm	Add chorizo, mushrooms and olives to the casserole. Return to oven.
7.00pm	Serve.

BAKED SALMON WITH DILL

1 x 1.5Kg (approx.) whole salmon, washed
3 tablespoons dry white wine
75g butter
2 bay leaves
Salt and pepper
1 bunch fresh dill

To serve: salad leaves, sliced cucumber, lemon slices and shop bought mayonnasie. I like Hellmann's.

Pre-heat oven to 140C (120 fan), Gas 1.

Remove head and tail from salmon, if preferred.

Place salmon in centre of a very large sheet of generously buttered tin foil.

Put remaining butter, bay leaves and chopped dill stalks inside body of fish.

Season well with salt and pepper, then pour wine over fish. Wrap foil over salmon to make a loose but sealed package. Stand package in a roasting tin.

Bake in centre of oven for 2 hours 10 minutes.

Turn off heat, remove salmon and leave wrapped, until completely cold.

Carefully remove fish from roasting tin. Unwrap and transfer to a board. Skin the salmon and remove any dark brown flesh by scraping it away.

Arrange salmon on a flat serving platter, joining two halves back together if you have cut fish in half.

Sprinkle chopped dill over salmon and use cucumber to decorate.

To serve, garnish edge of dish with a few salad leaves and the lemon slices.

Serve with the mayonnaise.

PORK & CHORIZO STEW

700g lean shoulder pork, cut into cubes
2 rashers lean back bacon, chopped
2 onions, peeled and roughly chopped
1 stick celery, chopped
3 large cloves garlic, chopped
1x 440ml can dry cider
8 tablespoons olive oil
3 tablespoons tomato purée
1 tablespoon red wine vinegar
Salt and black pepper
Large bunch fresh thyme or 1 tablespoon dried thyme
50g plain flour
500ml chicken stock
100g button mushrooms, halved
230g chorizo, skinned and sliced thickly
About 12 pimento stuffed olives
To serve: a selection of bread rolls

Place pork, bacon, onions and garlic into a large bowl.

Pour over cider, 3 tablespoons olive oil, tomato purée, vinegar and a seasoning of salt and pepper.

Add fresh thyme, tied into a bundle, or sprinkle in the dried thyme.
Stir thoroughly to mix. Cover bowl with cling film or a dinner plate.

Leave to marinate in fridge for 24 hours.

Pre-heat oven to 170C (150 fan), Gas 3.

Strain off marinade and reserve.

Heat 4 tablespoons olive oil in a large casserole.
Brown meat etc. on all sides, in batches, adding a little more oil if necessary.
Remove and set aside, using a slotted spoon.

Stir flour into oil remaining in pan and cook for about 1 minute.
Blend tomato purée into reserved marinade, with the red wine vinegar.

Gradually, add this liquid, to casserole, with the chicken stock, stirring constantly, over a medium heat, until liquid boils and produces a sauce. Use a balloon whisk if necessary. Simmer sauce for 1 minute, stirring.

Replace meat. Cover with a tightly fitting lid and return to boiling point.

Transfer to oven and cook for 2 hours, until meat is tender.

Meanwhile, fry chorizo slices in a non-stick frying pan, until browned.

Drain on absorbent kitchen paper and add to casserole with the mushrooms and olives.

Return casserole to oven for 15 minutes, covered.

Serve with bread rolls and salad.

SPINACH & AVOCADO SALAD

210g fresh young spinach leaves
½ a cucumber
1 bag radishes
1 large avocado, Hass, if available
60ml olive oil
30ml red wine vinegar
2 teaspoons Dijon mustard
Salt and black pepper
4 tablespoons pumpkin seeds

Pull off and discard any tough stalks from spinach.

Rinse spinach in several changes of cold water.

Drain well. Dry on absorbent kitchen paper and place in a salad bowl. Peel cucumber.

With a swivel type vegetables peeler, shave off "ribbons" of cucumber and add to bowl.

Wash radishes. Top and tail, halve each radish and add to bowl.

Peel, stone and roughly chop avocado. Add to bowl.

In a medium size bowl, combine: oil, vinegar, mustard and a seasoning of salt and pepper. Whisk to combine. Taste and adjust seasoning, if necessary.

When ready to serve but not before or salad will wilt, pour dressing over salad.

Toss to coat.

Serve sprinkled with pumpkin seeds.

LEMON, RASPBERRY & KIWI FRUIT PAVLOVA

4 large egg whites, at room temperature
225g caster sugar
1 teaspoon cornflour
1 tablespoon white wine vinegar

For the topping
300ml double cream
250ml crème fraiche, low fat version if preferred
3 heaped teaspoons finest quality lemon curd, optional
350g raspberries, fresh or frozen
2 kiwi fruits, peeled and sliced

Use a 20cm. dinner plate or saucepan lid to trace a circle onto a piece of baking parchment. Arrange, upside down, on a greased baking sheet. There is no need to grease paper.

Heat oven to 150C (130 fan), Gas 2.

Make meringue base. In a large clean bowl whisk egg whites until they stand in stiff peaks.

Add sugar, one dessertspoon at a time, whisking, after each addition, until a glossy, stiff meringue results.

Mix the cornflour and vinegar to a smooth paste, fold into meringue using a metal spoon and a cutting motion.
With aid of a spatula, turn mixture onto centre of paper.

Use a large palette knife to spread meringue to fit circle and draw edges into peaks. Turn oven down to 140C (120 fan), Gas 1.

Put pavlova into oven, just above centre and cook for 1½ hours.
Turn oven off and leave in oven for 2 hours, to cool completely, or overnight.

Prepare topping, which can be done up to 2 hours before serving and held in fridge. In a large bowl, whip cream until floppy. Fold in crème fraiche and lemon curd, if using.

Add half the raspberries. At this stage, you have the option of transferring the filling to a jug, and storing in the fridge. (a plastic jug takes up less fridge space than a bowl).

When ready to serve, or up to 1 hour before guests arrive, as long as you have space in fridge, arrange pavlova on a large plate or tray. Pile cream filling, on top.

Decorate with remaining raspberries and kiwi fruit, allowing some fruit to spill over onto edge of plate.

Serve

MENU 12

Slow Cooked Lunch or Supper

Serves 6
A little effort required: Ready in 3 hours approx.

* Roast Belly of Pork with Roasted Apples, Onions & Cider Gravy
* Mashed Potatoes
* Buttery Cabbage with Caraway Seeds
* Steamed Syrup Sponge

Belly of pork is a wonderful joint to serve. The layers of fat, roast down slowly, resulting in a succulent roast with a rich flavour.

Both the pork and syrup sponge are fairly easy to prepare but need slow cooking, leaving you time to do other things. About 40 minutes before service you will need to cook the potatoes and make the cider gravy. A real feast that is particularly welcome on a cold winter's day.

COOK'S HINTS & TIPS

To get good crackling, pork skin must be allowed to dry out, in the fridge, for a minimum of one day, preferably two. Salt skin, just before cooking, using both types of salt. Fine salt draws out moisture and coarse sea salt creates a crisp crackling.

The pudding is really easy to make and tastes wonderful! Ensure you seal pudding well and tie string round tightly to prevent any water from entering pudding basin.

SIMPLE TIME PLAN

To eat at: **8pm**
One or preferably two days in advance, prepare pork. Trim off and discard any excess fat from underside of belly. Wipe skin dry with kitchen paper.
Refrigerate, uncovered.

5.00pm	Remove pork from fridge. Pre-heat oven to 180C (160 fan), Gas 4/5. Prepare apples and onions.
5.20pm	Prepare pork for oven. Put in oven to roast on apples and onions
5.30pm	Make pudding. Put water onto boil.
5.45pm	Put sealed pudding in steamer and steam. Now you are free to do other things. Ensure you top up pan, regularly, with boiling water, if necessary, as the pudding cooks in the steam.
7.20pm	Peel the potatoes. Cook and mash. Keep warm.
7.45pm	Remove pork and set aside to rest for at least 15 minutes.
7.50pm	Make gravy. Prepare and cook cabbage.
8.00pm	Serve.

ROAST BELLY OF PORK WITH ONIONS & GRAVY

1 piece boned pork belly, about 2kg, skin finely scored on diagonal
2 large onions cut into wedges
3 large Cox's apples, cored and sliced into thick wedges
½ bunch fresh thyme
Sea salt and fine salt
Freshly ground white pepper
2 tablespoons olive oil

Trim off and discard any excess fat from underside of pork belly. Wipe skin dry.
Chill in fridge, uncovered, on a plate for up to 2 days.

Rub a tablespoon of fine salt all over skin, pressing it into score lines.
Grind sea salt all over skin.

Pre-heat oven to 180C (160 fan), Gas 4/5.

Put onion and apple wedges into a heavy roasting tin with the thyme and olive oil.
Season, with a little salt, and pepper. Using spoons, toss apples and onions to coat with the oil.
Put pork on top of onions and apples and wipe skin dry again.

Sprinkle with a further teaspoon fine salt, massaging into skin, using your hands.
Put roasting tin into oven, towards the top and roast for 1½ hours.
Increase temperature, to 210C (200 fan), Gas 6½.

Roast for a further 45 minutes to 1 hour until crackling crisps.
Remove pork from oven and allow to rest in a warm place for approx. 15 minutes.
Remove crackling and cut into thin strips, carve meat crossways into neat slices.

Serve with some of the onion and apple, accompanied by the gravy.

CIDER GRAVY

150ml dry cider
450ml chicken stock
4 teaspoons cornflour

Transfer any sediment and a little of the fat left in roasting tin, to a saucepan
(you are far less likely to get lumps this way!).
Add cider and stock. Bring slowly to the boil. Simmer for 10 minutes. Remove pan from heat.

In a mug, mix cornflour to a smooth paste with a little cold water.
Gradually stir blended cornflour, into stock mixture.
Bring pan to the boil, stirring constantly until a perfect gravy results.
Continue to simmer gently for 3-4 minutes.
Serve with pork, onions and apples.

MASHED POTATOES

1.25kg potatoes peeled and cut into large chunks
2 tablespoons extra virgin olive oil
200ml full fat milk, warmed
3 tablespoons crème fraiche
Salt and black pepper

Cook potatoes in a large pan of lightly-salted water for 15-20 minutes, until tender.

Drain potatoes well, through a colander. Leave in colander to "steam" uncovered for 2-3 minutes.

Return potatoes to pan. Mash well, using a potato masher. Reserve 2 tablespoons of the warmed milk.

Add remaining milk, a seasoning of salt and pepper, crème fraiche, and oil.

Beat with a wooden spoon, or a hand held electric mixer, until light and fluffy.
Turn into warmed vegetable dish.
Pour reserved milk over surface.

Cover with foil and place in low oven to keep warm. Mashed potato will hold like this for up to 1 hour without spoiling.

BUTTERY CABBAGE WITH CARAWAY SEEDS

1 large Savoy cabbage, outside leaves removed, washed
Approx. 300ml boiling water
½ teaspoon salt
50g butter
2 teaspoons caraway seeds

Simmer shredded cabbage in lightly-salted boiling water for 5-6 minutes, until cooked to your liking. Drain and return to pan.
Add butter and toss to coat.
Turn into vegetable dish and serve immediately, sprinkled with caraway seeds.

STEAMED SYRUP PUDDING

You will need a 1.2 litre pudding basin and a double layer of either, tin foil, or greaseproof paper, measuring approx. 40cm x 30cm, greased with butter. You will also need string.

Note: the butter must be at warm room temperature for this recipe so that it mixes easily, so remember to get it out of fridge early.

Butter for greasing
3 tablespoons golden syrup
175g self raising flour
1 teaspoon baking powder
175g softened butter
3 large eggs
175g soft light brown sugar or caster sugar
To serve: 3 extra tablespoons golden syrup mixed with 1 tablespoon water, for pouring over steamed pudding.
Custard, cream or ice cream

Butter the pudding basin, then, using a spoon, warmed in hot water, measure 3 tablespoons syrup into it.

Sift the flour and baking powder into a large mixing bowl.

Add the softened butter with the beaten eggs and sugar.

Using a hand held electric beater, beat for about 2 minutes until light and fluffy. It helps if you stand the bowl on a damp dish cloth to stop it slipping.

Turn the mixture into the greased pudding basin. Level surface.

Place tin foil or greaseproof over pudding, making a pleat in the centre to allow pudding to rise.

Tie string tightly, round the rim, then trim off any excess with scissors.

Place pudding in steamer, fitted over a saucepan of simmering water. The water should come about half way up the pan.

Cover with a tightly fitting lid and steam pudding for 2 hours, topping up water level with boiling water, when necessary.

To serve, warm remaining golden syrup in a small pan with the water.

Remove foil, loosen pudding round edges with a round bladed knife.
Turn out onto a warmed plate.

Pour warmed syrup over pudding and serve immediately with custard, cream or ice cream.

MENU 13
Entertain from the Freezer

Serves 6
Some skill required: Ready in 3½ hours approx.

* Chicken Liver Pâté
* Lamb Hot Pot with Sweet Potato Mash
* Lemon Cheesecake

Remember to transfer dishes from freezer to refrigerator 2 days in advance of party.

Ask the butcher to dice the lamb for you.

If guests are staying overnight, it makes sense to have one course stored away in the freezer. Re-heat to piping hot, according to directions given.

COOK'S HINTS & TIPS

Ensure each recipe is completely cold before packing and freezing.
Remember that food expands on freezing, so leave "head room" in containers.

Freeze food in containers with tightly fitting lids or in sealed plastic bags, removing as much air as possible first. Label clearly, to prevent disasters!
I once tried to serve chicken stock, thinking it was vanilla ice cream!

To peel shallots easily, place them in a bowl. Cover with boiling water and set aside for 10 minutes. Drain and cover with cold water. Drain and slip off skins.

Remove chicken liver pâté from fridge about 1 hour before serving as the pâté needs to be served at room temperature.

Although gelatine can be tricky to freeze, this cheesecake freezes well. Just ensure it is de- frosted slowly in the fridge.

SIMPLE TIME PLAN

Assuming dishes have been frozen and de-frosted, allow yourself about 1½ hours to re-heat and organise meal.

Remember to make toast to serve with the pâté.

CHICKEN LIVER PÂTÉ

125g butter, softened
2 cloves garlic, peeled and crushed
1 bay leaf
1 tablespoon freshly chopped parsley
450g chicken livers, trimmed, and chopped roughly
3 tablespoons dry sherry
Salt and black pepper

To Serve: Freshly made toast and butter

Melt half the butter in a large frying pan.
Add garlic, bay leaf, parsley, and chicken livers.
Fry over high heat for 5 minutes, stirring occasionally.
Set aside to cool.
Remove bay leaf. Transfer contents of pan to a food processor fitted with metal blade.
Blend until smooth. Transfer to large mixing bowl.
Add sherry to frying pan. Bring to the boil, scraping any sediment from base of pan.
Pass through sieve, into liver mixture.
Beat in remaining butter and season to taste. Divide mixture between 6 ramekin dishes.
Cool, then pack and freeze.
Transfer to fridge 24 hours before serving.

LAMB HOT POT WITH SWEET POTATO MASH

2 tablespoons corn or vegetable oil
900g lean shoulder or best end & middle neck of lamb cut into 2.5cm cubes
2 tablespoons plain flour
12 shallots, peeled
2 celery stalks, chopped
3 carrots, sliced
1 medium onion, peeled
6 sprigs fresh thyme, tied into a bundle
2 bay leaves
750ml lamb or chicken stock
Salt and black pepper
100g button mushrooms, halved
175g broad beans

To serve: freshly chopped parsley

Pre-heat oven to 150C (130 fan), Gas 2.
Toss lamb in seasoned flour.
Heat oil in a large, heavy-based frying pan.
Add lamb, in batches and fry until golden on all sides.
Transfer to a large casserole dish using a slotted spoon.
Add shallots, celery and carrots to frying pan and fry until lightly browned.
Transfer to casserole dish.
Add whole onion, thyme, bay leaves and stock.
Cover with a tightly fitting lid and cook for 2½ to 3 hours, stirring occasionally, until lamb is tender. Cool, pack and freeze.

FROM FROZEN

Transfer frozen casserole to fridge and leave to de-frost for 2 days.
When ready to re-heat, transfer lamb and juices to casserole dish.
Remove and discard whole onion.

Re-heat, covered, in pre-heated oven 180C (160 fan), Gas 4, for approx. 1 hour. stirring half-way through.

Cook beans in a little salted water, for 10 minutes, until tender. Stir into the casserole, with the raw mushrooms. Return to oven for 15 minutes. Stir.
Check contents of casserole are piping hot, before serving sprinkled with the chopped parsley.

SWEET POTATO MASH

900g sweet potatoes, peeled and cut into chunks
Juice ½ orange
50g butter
2 tablespoons freshly chopped parsley
Salt and black pepper

Cook potatoes in a large pan of boiling, salted water for 15 minutes until very tender when tested with a sharp knife.

Drain well and allow to steam dry for 5 minutes.

Return to pan and mash with a potato masher.

Add orange juice, and a seasoning of salt and pepper.

Beat well with a wooden spoon.

Cool completely.

Pack in a labelled, airtight container and freeze.

When ready to use, remove sweet potato mash from freezer 2 days before required.

De-frost in refrigerator.

Transfer de-frosted potato to a suitable, oven proof dish. Stir in parsley.

Cover with foil or a lid.

Re-heat until piping hot in a pre-heated oven 180C (160 fan), Gas 4 for approx. one hour.
Stir and re-cover once half-way through. Serve.

LEMON CHEESECAKE

200g digestive biscuits, finely crushed
75g butter, melted
15ml powdered gelatine
100g cream cheese
1 large egg, separated
150g natural Greek yoghurt
Grated rind and juice 1 large lemon
75g caster sugar
150ml double cream
15ml lemon curd

To serve: fresh raspberries, optional, but nice. Single cream

You will need 1x 22cm, loose-bottomed or spring-form cake tin, lightly greased with a little of the butter.

In a medium size saucepan, mix biscuit crumbs into melted butter. Press mixture into prepared cake tin, to line base.

In a small bowl, sprinkle gelatine over 45ml cold water and set aside for 10 minutes to soak.

Place bowl over a pan of simmering water, ensuring bowl does not touch water. Stir until gelatine has dissolved. Set aside, until just warm.

Place cream cheese, egg yolk, Greek yoghurt, rind and juice of lemon and caster sugar into a food processor, fitted with the metal blade.

Blend until smooth.

Transfer mixture to large mixing bowl.

Whip cream until it just holds its shape.

Fold dissolved gelatine, whipped cream and lemon curd into cheese mixture until evenly distributed.

In a separate clean bowl, whisk egg white until stiff.

Fold into cheese mixture. Pour evenly onto biscuit base and chill in fridge until completely set.

Remove from tin. Pack, label and freeze or serve immediately, decorated with fresh raspberries, if using.

To Serve from Frozen:
Transfer cheesecake from freezer to fridge at least 24 hours before serving.

Decorate with fresh raspberries and serve with single cream.

MENU 14
Celebration Dinner Party
Serves 6

* Easy Carbonara
* Steamed Broccoli & Asparagus
* Chocolate Biscuit Cake or Sliced Melon with Blackberries

Get ahead and prepare the chocolate cake up to two days in advance. It also freezes well, de-frost, overnight in fridge.

Serve this quick and easy menu for family birthday celebrations. The carbonara is a useful recipe to have up your sleeve when guests arrive unexpectedly and stay for supper!

COOK'S HINTS & TIPS
Carbonara is filling, so guests may not be up to eating much of a pudding. You may like to include an alternative dessert of sliced melon of your choice, with cultivated blackberries.
The carbonara can be prepared while the vegetables are steaming.

Break broccoli into florettes and clean asparagus, breaking off woody stems where they snap naturally.

Ensure guests are at the table before you assemble carbonara.

SIMPLE TIME PLAN
To eat at: **8pm.**
Assuming chocolate biscuit cake has been made in advance.

7.30pm	Assemble ingredients for carbonara.
7.40pm	Put vegetables on to steam.
7.45pm	Cook pasta in boiling, salted water. Meanwhile prepare and cook vegetables and sauce for pasta.
7.55pm	Assemble carbonara. Drain vegetables.
7.55pm	Serve. Prepare melon and blackberries, if including, between courses.

EASY CARBONARA

500g tagliatelle or spaghetti
2 onions, chopped
275g smoked back bacon, chopped
2 courgettes, topped, tailed and diced
2 tablespoons olive oil
3 large egg yolks
300 ml double cream
75g Parmesan or Rigatoni cheese, grated
3 tablespoons freshly chopped parsley

Cook tagliatelle or spaghetti, in a very large pan of boiling, salted water for about 9 minutes, until tender, or as directed on the pack.

Meanwhile, heat the oil in a large saucepan. Cook onion and bacon, over a moderate heat, for about 8 minutes, stirring frequently, until onion softens and is lightly golden. Add courgettes and continue to cook, stirring for 5 minutes.

In a mixing bowl, beat together egg yolks and cream. Add a seasoning of salt and plenty of pepper.

Drain pasta and return to pan. Add onion mixture, add cream mixture. Stir over low heat for 1-2 minutes, to gently heat through. Turn into a large, heated bowl and serve immediately, topped with the grated parmesan and chopped parsley.

CHOCOLATE BISCUIT CAKE

125g butter
1x 397g can condensed milk
150g bar plain chocolate, broken into pieces
250g digestive biscuits, broken into pieces
6 ready to eat dried apricots, chopped

To Serve: Vanilla Ice Cream

You will need 1x 20cm round shallow, loose bottomed cake tin.

Grease cake tin, with a little of the butter. Line base with greaseproof paper. Lightly grease paper.

Put remaining butter into a large heat proof bowl, with the condensed milk and chocolate. Put bowl over a pan of simmering water, but do not allow bowl to touch water.
Stir until melted.
Remove from heat. Stir in biscuit pieces and apricots, until well coated.
Pour mixture into cake tin. Cool, then chill for at least 2 hours.
Pack and freeze cooled cake, if required.
Turn cake out onto a bread board and remove grease proof.

Serve in small pieces with ice cream.

MENU 15
Saturday Lunch

Serves 6
Some skill needed: Ready in 2¼ hours approx.

With cream in both the potato dish and the dessert, there is no need to serve a starter.
Prepare crème brulée, at least a day in advance.
You may like to use egg whites to make a pavlova.
A plate of fresh fruit would make a good alternative dessert.

* Sausage Casserole
* Potato Dauphinoise with Onion
* Swede & Carrot Crush
* Crème Brulée

Good British sausages are just about everyone's favourite. If possible, buy two different varieties, from a reputable butcher, or alternatively look for supermarket's finest. You may pay a little more but, with sausages, you really do get what you pay for!

The potato dauphinoise is delicious with this casserole.

The crème brulée recipe makes enough to fill 6 small ramekins.

Granulated, demerera or soft brown sugar may be used for the topping of the crème Brulées. You need enough to completely cover the creamy base.

COOK'S HINTS & TIPS
If potatoes are browning too quickly, cover dish, removing foil for last 10 minutes.
It is important to cook crème brulées in a water bath, to ensure they don't overheat.

SIMPLE TIME PLAN
To eat at: **1.45pm**

12.00am	Pre-heat oven to 170C (150 fan), Gas 3. Prepare potato dauphinoise.
12.05pm	Simmer potatoes for 10 minutes.
12.20pm	Turn potatoes into buttered dish. Put into oven.
12.25pm	Prepare swede and carrot purée. Cook vegetables. Mash, turn into vegetable tureen and keep warm.
1.00pm	Prepare sausage casserole. Fry coriander seeds, vegetables and sausages. Assemble casserole. Bring to boil.
1.15pm	Transfer casserole to oven.
1.45pm	Serve.

SAUSAGE CASSEROLE

1 teaspoon coriander seeds, crushed
5 tablespoons olive oil
16 large, good quality pork sausages
2 medium red onions, finely chopped
2 celery sticks, chopped
1 carrot, sliced
2 garlic cloves, chopped
4x 400g cans chopped tomatoes
2 tablespoons tomato purée
2 teaspoons Demerara sugar
2 bay leaves
300ml chicken stock, or use stock from cooking swede and carrots
2 tablespoons Dijon mustard
Salt and pepper
2x400g cans red kidney beans, drained and rinsed
Salt and pepper
2 tablespoons freshly chopped parsley
To serve: a choice of mustards

Pre-heat oven to 170C (150 fan), Gas 3.

Heat a large frying pan and dry fry coriander seeds for 1 minute, to release flavour.

Set aside.

In the same pan heat 2 tablespoons oil and brown sausages all over, over high heat. You may have to do this in 2 batches. Set aside.

Heat remaining oil, in a large casserole dish.

Gently fry onion, celery and carrot for 10 minutes, until softened.

Add garlic and cook for 1 minute.

Add tomatoes with tomato purée and Demerara sugar.

Stir in coriander seeds, stock, mustard, sausages and bay leaves.

Add a little salt and some freshly ground black pepper.

Bring to the boil. Cover with a lid.

Transfer to oven and cook for 40 minutes, below potatoes.

Stir in beans, return to oven for 15 minutes.

Stir in parsley and serve, accompanied by the mustards.

POTATO DAUPHINOISE WITH ONION

1 tablespoon corn oil
1 x 300g packet freshly chopped onion or 2 onions, peeled and chopped
50g butter, plus extra for greasing
300ml double cream
300ml semi-skimmed milk
A few sprigs fresh thyme
3 bay leaves
1.25kg floury potatoes such as Maris Piper
Salt and pepper

Pre-heat the oven to 170C (150 fan), Gas 3.

Grease an ovenproof dish about 23cm x 25cm x 5cm deep with a little butter.

Heat oil in a frying pan. Add onions and cook over moderate heat, stirring frequently for approx. 10 minutes until onions soften.

Meanwhile, put butter, cream, milk, thyme and bay leaves into a large saucepan. Season with salt and pepper and bring to the boil. Simmer gently for 10 minutes.

Cut peeled potatoes into very thin slices using a sharp knife.

Strain infused milk mixture into a jug. Pour this liquid back into pan and add potatoes and onions.

Gently cook over medium heat for 10 minutes, stirring frequently. Tip into dish.

Cook uncovered, in centre of oven for approx. 1½ hours, until potatoes in centre are tender when pierced with a sharp knife. Serve immediately.

SWEDE & CARROT CRUSH

900g swedes, peeled
2 large carrots, peeled
600ml vegetable stock
1 tablespoon freshly chopped coriander
Salt and pepper
50g butter

Dice swede and carrot, separately.

Put swede into a large saucepan, cover with vegetable stock and bring to boil.

Cover with a lid and simmer for 20 minutes.

Add carrot, return to boil and continue to simmer, covered, for approximately 15 minutes, until vegetables are tender.

Drain through a colander, reserving stock, to use in the casserole.

Mash vegetables to a purée, adding butter and a little of the reserved stock, if necessary, but don't make purée too wet.

Season, with a little salt and pepper.

Transfer to vegetable dish, cover and keep warm until ready to serve.

CRÈME BRULÉE

NOTE: These desserts may be made up to 2 days in advance. Once cold, cover with cling film and chill in fridge.

500ml double cream
1 vanilla pod
100g caster sugar
6 large egg yolks
9 teaspoons Demerera sugar

Pre-heat oven to 140C (120 fan), Gas 1.
Pour cream into a saucepan.
Split vanilla pod lengthways and scrape seeds into cream.
Chop empty vanilla pod into small pieces and add to cream.
Bring to boil.
Lower heat and simmer for 5 minutes.

In a large mixing bowl, beat sugar and egg yolks, using an electric whisk, until pale and creamy.

Pour boiling cream onto egg yolks and continue to whisk on low speed, until mixture thickens to consistency of light custard.
Strain through a sieve into a large jug.
Fill 6-8 ramekins with this mixture.

Place ramekins in a large roasting tin and pour enough hot water carefully into tin to come halfway up sides of ramekins.

Place in centre of oven and bake for 30-40 minutes, until just set but still a bit wobbly in centre.

Remove from water bath and cool.
Sprinkle 1½ teaspoons sugar onto each crème brulée.
Caramelise with a mini blow torch or under a pre-heated hot grill.

Allow to cool slightly before serving.

Alternatively, allow to cool completely.

Chill in fridge, until ready to serve.

MENU 16
Teenager's Party
Serves 6
Fairly easy: Ready in 1 hour approx.

* Cajun Chicken Fajitas
* Easy Guacamole
* Cherry Clafoutis

Everyone loves simple-to-make fajitas. Just remember to be organised with everything to hand, before you start to cook.

The clafoutis dessert is a delicious batter pudding with fresh fruit and is much easier to make than it sounds. De-frosted, frozen cherries work well in this recipe.

COOK'S HINTS & TIPS

Ensure oil is really hot before you add chicken so that it sizzles and browns quickly. You will probably need to cook the chicken in two batches.

To help prevent guacamole from discolouring, retain stone from avocado and put it into centre of the dip when you "hold" it in fridge. Remove stone, before serving.

The biscuit crumbs, used in the clafoutis recipe help with the texture of the cooked pudding. If preferred, however, you can leave them out.

SIMPLE TIME PLAN

To eat at: **7.30pm**

6.15pm	Prepare batter for clafoutis and set aside.
6.35pm	Prepare accompaniments to fajitas, except guacamole. Arrange on table.
7.00pm	Prepare and chill guacamole
7.10pm	Prepare and cook chicken fajitas. Keep warm. Pre-heat oven to 220C (200 fan), Gas 7.
7.20pm	Heat cherries for clafoutis. Warm tortillas, as directed on pack.
7.30pm	Drain cherries, reserving juice. Return cherries to dish.
	Pour over batter and return to oven. Cook the clafoutis while you eat the fajitas. Just remember to set the timer!

CAJUN CHICKEN FAJITAS

Approx. 6 tablespoons olive oil
5 large chicken breast fillets, cut into 2.5cm.dice
1 tablespoon blackened Cajun seasoning
2 red peppers, de-seeded and thickly sliced
1 yellow pepper, de-seeded and thickly sliced
2 red onions, peeled and cut into thin wedges
2 cloves garlic, crushed
6 flour tortillas warmed according to instructions on packet

To serve with the tortillas:
½ iceberg lettuce, shredded
4 medium ripe tomatoes, de-seeded and chopped
1 recipe guacamole
120ml (approx.) sour cream
1 lime, cut into wedges

Heat 3 tablespoons of the oil in a large, non-stick frying pan.

Toss the chicken in the Cajun seasoning to coat. (You may need to cook the chicken in two batches).

Fry each batch for 5-6 minutes until lightly browned on all sides and cooked through.

Tip cooked chicken onto a plate and keep warm.

Add remaining oil to pan, add peppers and onions to pan and stir fry until softened and lightly browned, about 5-7 minutes.

Add garlic, and continue to fry for 1minute.

To serve, pile vegetables onto a warmed oval serving plate.

Top with fried, spicy chicken.

Garnish with lime wedges.

Place plate in centre of table surrounded by warmed tortillas, bowl of shredded lettuce, small bowl of chopped tomatoes, guacamole and soured cream.

Place a teaspoon beside each "accompaniment".

Invite guests to fill tortillas with a little of everything, Mexican style.

EASY GUACAMOLE

2 medium size, ripe tomatoes
3 ripe avocados, Hass variety are good
1 medium red onion, roughly chopped
1 fat clove garlic, crushed
Juice 1 lime
½ teaspoon chilli powder
Salt

Put the tomatoes into a bowl. Cover with boiling water and set aside for a few minutes. Drain and cool for a few minutes.

Slip off the skins, scoop out and discard seeds. Roughly chop tomato flesh.

Halve avocados. Remove stone. Cut each avocado in half, length ways. Peel each quarter. Roughly chop avocado flesh and put into a food processor, fitted with the metal blade.

Process until finely chopped.

Add onion, garlic, tomatoes, lime juice and chilli powder. Process until roughly blended. Transfer to a serving bowl. Add a seasoning of salt to taste and a little extra chilli powder, if necessary.

Cover and chill for 15 minutes to allow flavours to mingle, before serving.

CHERRY CLAFOUTIS

For the filling
Butter for greasing
450g fresh, stoned, dark cherries or ripe plums, washed, stoned and quartered
1 level tablespoon granulated sugar
2 tablespoons water
2 tablespoons crushed digestive biscuits, about 3 biscuits

For the batter
3 large eggs
60g caster sugar
½ teaspoon vanilla extract
300ml whole milk
60g plain flour
To Serve: sieved icing sugar for dredging, reserved cherry juice, vanilla ice cream

You will need a dish, approx. 27cm x 18cm x 5cm deep, lightly greased.

Pre-heat oven to 220C (200 fan), Gas 7.

Combine cherries, or plums, sugar and water.

Place in the lightly-greased oven proof dish.

Put in oven for 8-10 minutes, until cherries are hot.

Drain cherries, reserving juice.

Meanwhile, prepare batter. In a large mixing bowl, or jug, and using an electric whisk, beat eggs and sugar, until combined. Whisk in milk and vanilla extract, briefly.

Put flour, into a large mixing bowl. Make well in centre. Gradually whisk in liquid ingredients to form a smooth batter. Beat for 1 minute.

Set aside to rest, for 5-10 minutes.

Mix hot cherries with biscuit crumbs.

Pour batter over cherries.

Bake immediately, for approximately 30 minutes, until well risen, golden and firm in centre.

Leave to cool for about 5 minutes before serving, dredged with icing sugar.

Accompany with ice cream, and reserved cherry juice.

MENU 17
Vegetarian
Serves 6
Some Skill required: Ready in: 1½ hours approx.

* Sweet Potato, Mozzarella & Pesto Tart
* Soda Bread
* Jelly Trifles

Soda bread does not keep well, so make on day of party.

If possible, make trifles in the morning or a day in advance and serve, well chilled. Bake bread above vegetable tart as it cooks at a slightly higher temperature.

The coleslaw recipe from Menu 3 makes a good addition to this menu.

COOK'S HINTS & TIPS
Assemble all ingredients for each dish before you start recipe.

You could blend remains of jar of pesto, into some Greek yoghurt for a dip to serve, with sticks of carrot, celery and red pepper, as guests arrive.

For the soda bread: if you are going to sour the milk yourself, simply stir 1 tablespoon lemon juice into the milk, before starting on the recipe.

SIMPLE TIME PLAN
To eat at: 7.00pm

By 11am	Make trifles. Chill in fridge.
5.25pm	Pre-heat oven to 220C (200 fan), Gas 7.
5.30pm	Prepare the vegetable and mozzarella tart. Chill tart.
5.50pm	Prepare dough for soda bread.
6.15pm	Bake bread toward top of oven and tart below.
6.20pm	Prepare coleslaw, if including. Chill in the fridge.
6.45pm	Remove bread. Transfer to cooling rack.
6.50pm	Remove tart, checking that sweet potato is tender, return to oven for a few minutes, if necessary.
7.05pm	Serve.

SWEET POTATO, MOZZARELLA AND PESTO TART

500g puff pastry, de-frosted, if frozen
2 tablespoons milk
4 tablespoons olive oil, approx
2 red skinned onions, chopped
1 large red pepper, de-seeded and chopped
1 teaspoon dried mixed herbs
½ x 190g jar classic basil pesto
1 large red chilli, de seeded and finely chopped
300g mozzarella
3 ripe tomatoes
1 medium sweet potato, about 300g
Salt and pepper

Pre heat oven to 200C (180 fan), Gas 7.

On a lightly floured board, roll pastry into a rectangle, approximately 25cm x 30cm.

Transfer to a large baking sheet.

With a sharp knife, score a border inside the pastry, about 2.5cm width from the edge.

Brush the border with the milk and chill.

In a large frying pan, heat 2 tablespoons of the oil .

Fry onions for about 10 minutes, stirring over medium heat, until softened and lightly golden.

Add red pepper and mixed herbs.

Transfer to a mixing bowl and stir in pesto sauce and chopped chilli, just to combine.

Thinly slice the mozzarella, tomatoes, and sweet potato.

Remove pastry from fridge and spread onion mixture evenly over inner rectangle.

Overlap mozzarella, tomatoes and sweet potato in neat rows. You will need to build these ingredients into an even mound.

Season, with a little salt, and pepper. Finish with a drizzle of oil.

Bake for 30-35 minutes, until pastry is golden and sweet potato is tender when pierced with a knife.

Leave to cool for a couple of minutes before serving with coleslaw and bread.

SODA BREAD

350g seed and grain bread flour, or wholemeal flour
350g plain white flour
1 level teaspoon table salt
50g lard + extra for greasing
3 level teaspoons bicarbonate of soda
6 level teaspoons cream of tartar
2 level teaspoons caster sugar
450ml buttermilk, or soured milk, approx

Pre-heat oven to 220C (200 fan), Gas 7.
In a large mixing bowl, combine both types of flour and salt.
Rub in lard. Mix in bicarbonate of soda, cream of tartar and sugar.
Pour in buttermilk and lightly work into pliable dough, using floured hands.

Shape dough into a ball and place on a greased baking sheet.

Flatten slightly, then, with a sharp knife, mark a cross in the top but do not cut right through dough.

Dust lightly with wholemeal flour.

Bake immediately for approx. 30-35 minutes, until risen and lightly golden.

JELLY TRIFLES

Don't worry if there is a little icing on the sponges or fairy cakes. It adds something to the trifles!

2 x 135g packets vegetarian raspberry jelly, cut into cubes
24 seedless black grapes, washed, and halved plus extra to decorate
150g chocolate, or vanilla sponges, or fairy cakes, from the supermarket, cut into cubes

To serve: Greek yoghurt, whipped cream or crème fraiche

Make up jelly, according to pack instructions.

Set aside to cool completely. You only need 900ml of jelly for this recipe so pour the remaining 225ml into a dish and chill for another day.

Divide grapes between 6 wine glasses.
Arrange cake cubes on top.
Divide remaining 900ml cooled jelly between glasses, pouring it over cake and grapes.

Chill in fridge for at least 3 hours, or overnight.

Serve, topped with Greek yoghurt, whipped cream or crème fraiche, decorated with reserved grapes.

MENU 18
Entertain in a Flash
Serves 6
Very Easy: Ready in approx. 1¼ hours

* Oven-Fried Indian Chicken
* Little Gem & Tomato Salad.
* Naan Bread

* Fruits in Kirsch

COOK'S HINTS & TIPS
Choose the best chicken breasts you can afford as flavour and water content does vary somewhat! As always, you get what you pay for!

For a simple salad: combine leaves from 3 washed and drained little gem lettuce with a handful of rocket and a few cherry tomatoes. Toss in a mint vinaigrette made by combining, in a jug, 1 tablespoon white wine vinegar, and 3 tablespoons extra virgin olive oil. Add 2 chopped spring onions, 1 tablespoon freshly chopped mint leaves and a seasoning of salt and pepper. Whisk well, with a fork and pour over salad, on serving.

Buy naan bread from the supermarket and sprinkle with a little water before arranging on baking sheet and heating, in the oven.

SIMPLE TIME PLAN
To eat at: **8.15pm**

7.00pm	Prepare chicken. Set aside, once coated with spicy mixture, for 10 minutes. Pre-heat oven to 200C (180 fan), Gas 6.
7.15pm	Prepare salad and salad dressing. Chill both separately in fridge.
7.25pm	Cook the chicken.
7.30pm	Prepare dessert. Chill in fridge
7.55pm	Heat naan bread, on a baking sheet, for 5-7 minutes in the oven, below chicken.
8.15pm	Serve.

OVEN-FRIED INDIAN CHICKEN

You will need 6 metal skewers or 6 wooden skewers, soaked in water for 20 minutes before using to prevent them burning in the hot oven.

750g skinless chicken breast fillets, cut into bite size chunks
2 yellow peppers
2 tablespoons tandoori curry paste (I like Patak's Tikka Masala curry paste with coriander and lemon)
Juice ½ lemon
Olive oil

2 limes cut into wedges

Pre-heat oven to 200C (180 fan), Gas 6, or light BBQ.

Put pieces of chicken into a large mixing bowl.
Add tandoori paste, lemon juice and about 2 tablespoons olive oil.
Stir well to coat each piece of chicken with the spicy mixture.
Set aside for 10 minutes or if you have time, cover and chill, for 30 minutes
or overnight.
Lightly oil a large baking sheet.
De-seed peppers and cut into cubes about 2.5cm size.
When ready to cook, thread chicken and peppers on to skewers.
Stand on baking sheet.
Roast towards top of oven for 15-20 minutes until cooked and beginning to char. Turn skewers over, once, halfway through.

Alternatively BBQ skewers, for about 12 minutes turning frequently.

Serve the skewers with a wedge of lime.

FRUITS IN KIRSCH

4 oranges
225g fresh strawberries
1 medium size pineapple
1 tablespoon caster sugar, or to taste
6 tablespoons Kirsch or Cointreau

To serve: cream or ice cream

Peel oranges, removing all pith, then segment the fruits, holding them over a serving dish so that you catch any juice.
Put orange segments into a serving dish.
Wash, hull and slice strawberries, add to dish.
Peel and dice pineapple, discarding, central core. Add to dish.

Sprinkle with sugar and pour liqueur over.

Cover and chill for 15 minutes, or until ready to serve. (15 minutes is long enough for flavours to mingle).

Serve with cream or ice cream.

MENU 19

One Pot Supper

Serves 6
Some skill required: Ready in 4 hours approx.

* Lamb Tagine
* Couscous
* Lemon Meringue Pie

An easy menu, but allow plenty of time for the tagine, to cook slowly. If preferred, cook up to 2 days in advance. When completely cold, cover and chill in fridge for up to 2 days. Re-heat tagine in a covered casserole dish, in a pre-heated moderate oven, for approx. 1 hour, stirring halfway through.

COOKS HINTS & TIPS

You might like to try wholegrain couscous, which has a really good flavour.
The tagine is equally delicious served with jacket or mashed potatoes, rice or pasta so feel free to make your own choice.

SIMPLE TIME PLAN

To eat at: **8.00pm**

4.00pm	Pre-heat oven to 190C (170 fan), Gas 5. Prepare and cook pastry for pie. Prepare filling and meringue. Cook lemon meringue.
5.45pm	Remove lemon meringue pie and set aside. Reduce oven temperature to 150C (130 fan), Gas 2.
5.45pm	Prepare tagine.
6.00pm	Put tagine into oven.
7.45pm	Prepare the couscous according to instructions, on pack. Allow to stand for 10 minutes. Sir in the grated rind of 1 lemon, a handful chopped coriander, and 50g of sultanas.
7.55pm	Return lemon meringue pie to oven. Turn oven off.
8.00pm	Serve.

LAMB TAGINE

6 tablespoons olive oil
2 red onions, peeled and chopped
3 carrots, peeled and sliced
2 sticks celery, chopped
4 cloves garlic, chopped
1 teaspoon chilli powder
1 teaspoon ground turmeric
1 tablespoon ground smoked paprika
1 tablespoon fresh root ginger, peeled and grated
1kg diced leg or lean shoulder of lamb
2 tablespoons plain flour
Salt and black pepper
250g dates, stoned, then halved
100g ready to eat dried apricots, chopped
900ml lamb stock
2 cinnamon sticks
3 bay leaves
2 teaspoons honey

To garnish: chopped coriander or parsley

Pre-heat oven to 150C (130 fan), Gas 2.

In a large casserole, heat 3 tablespoons oil.
Add onions, carrots and celery and cook gently, stirring occasionally, for
10 minutes or until onions and celery soften.

Add garlic, chilli, turmeric, paprika and ginger. Stir well and continue to cook for 1-2 minutes.

In a large frying pan, heat remaining oil.
Toss meat in seasoned flour, easiest done on a large plate or in a plastic bag.
Add lamb to the hot oil, in the frying pan and sear on all sides until browned.

You will need to do this in batches.

Lift each batch of meat using a draining spoon and add to casserole
Add dates, apricots and lamb stock.
Add cinnamon sticks and bay leaves.

Stir well, adding a seasoning of salt and pepper.

Bring to the boil.

Cover with a lid and transfer to oven.

Cook for 2-2½ hours, until meat is meltingly tender.

Stir in honey.

Taste and adjust seasoning if necessary.

Serve garnished with the coriander or parsley, accompanied by couscous.

LEMON MERINGUE PIE

For the pastry
175g plain flour
40g cold butter, cubed
40g cold lard, cubed
Approx. 6 teaspoons cold water, to mix

For the filling
Grated rind & juice of 2 large lemons, at room temperature
275ml cold water
3 tablespoons cornflour
50g caster sugar
3 medium egg yolks
40g butter

For the meringue
3 medium egg whites
175g caster sugar

To serve: single cream or crème fraiche

You will need 1 x 23cm, loose bottomed, metal flan tin.

Pre-heat oven to 190C (170 fan), Gas 5.

Make the pastry. Put flour into a large mixing bowl.

Add butter and lard.

Rub fat into flour using finger tips and lifting ingredients as you go so as to incorporate air. Mixture needs to resemble fine bread crumbs.

Add water and work pastry into a ball of dough, using a round bladed knife, then hands.

Cover and chill for 20 minutes.

Roll to a round approx. 8mm larger, than circumference of flan tin.

Stand flat tin on baking sheet.

Lift pastry, on rolling pin and use to line flan tin, pressing it into sides and base. Chill again for 10 minutes, then use rolling pin to level top.

Prick base and sides, all over, with a fork. Bake blind for 15-20 minutes, until lightly golden.

Remove flan case from oven and immediately lower oven temperature to 150C (130 fan), Gas 2.

Now make the filling. Put lemon rind and juice into a medium saucepan with most of the measured water.

Use remaining water to mix cornflour to a smooth paste in a medium bowl.

Bring liquid in pan to the boil. Add it to cornflour mixture, stirring well.

Transfer mixture back into pan and bring to the boil, stirring continuously.

Simmer for 1 minute, stirring continuously, until thickened. Remove from heat and cool for 5 minutes.

Beat in egg yolks, one at a time. Beat in sugar. Pour into flan case and set aside.

Finally make meringue. Beat egg whites in a large clean mixing bowl until they form stiff peaks. This is easiest done with an electric mixer.

Beat in sugar a tablespoon at a time, until a glossy meringue results.

Spread meringue all over lemon filling, to very edge of pastry rim. Swirl up with knife.

Bake for approx. 45 minutes until meringue is tinged brown and is crisp on the outside and marshmallowy inside.

Remove from tin. Transfer to plate.

Serve warm or cold.

MENU 20
Festive Buffet
Serves 6
Some skill required: Ready in 2 hours 30 minutes approx.

You might like to offer a cheese board with fresh seasonal fruits as an alternative to the dessert. A salad, from one of the other meus, would also make a good addition.

* Cider Baked Gammon
* Cheddar Cheese & Broccoli Flan
* New Potatoes (see menu 1)
* Coleslaw with Blue Cheese Dressing
* A Selection of Olive & Sun Dried Tomato Bread
* Banoffi Pie

Try to get ahead and make the banoffi pie, up to one day in advance. Cover with cling film and chill in fridge.

COOKS HINTS & TIPS

Soak gammon overnight before cooking to get rid of excess salt. Should you forget, place gammon into a large casserole. Cover with cold water and bring to the boil. Drain off water and start recipe as directed. Buy bread ready made and pop into oven for 15 minutes before serving.

SIMPLE TIME PLAN

To eat at: **7.40pm** – assuming banoffi pie has been made in advance.

5.00pm	Drain gammon and put on to boil with prepared veg.
5.20pm	Simmer gammon.
5.25pm	Prepare pastry and line flan ring for cheese flan.
5.35pm	Chill pastry. Light oven for flan, 400F, 200C, Gas 6. Bake flan case blind.
5.35pm	Prepare coleslaw. Chill in fridge. Light oven for flan 200C (180 fan), Gas 6.
5.50pm	Complete broccoli & cheese flan. Bake.
6.10pm	Prepare salad, if using, but do not dress. Chill salad ingredients and dressing separately. Drain gammon. Wrap in foil, and bake gammon, below flan, reducing oven temperature to 180C (160 fan), Gas 4.
6.25pm	Prepare potatoes.
6.40pm	Remove flan. Keep warm.
6.45pm	Remove gammon. Prepare sugar glaze. Increase oven temperature to 200C (180 fan), Gas 6.
7.00pm	Skin and glaze gammon. Return to oven.
7.05pm	Cook the potatoes. Ready 7.25pm. Remove banoffi pie from tin. Arrange on a plate.
7.10pm	Enjoy drink with friends, remembering to check potatoes at 7.25pm.
7.35pm	Serve.

CIDER BAKED GAMMON

1.8kg middle gammon joint, smoked
2 medium onions, peeled and quartered
2 medium carrots, peeled and sliced
1 bay leaf
6 black peppercorns
2 sticks celery, chopped
600ml cider or apple juice
Cloves to garnish
2 tablespoons Dijon mustard
2 tablespoons Demerara sugar, approximately.

Soak gammon overnight in cold water.

Drain gammon, discard water.

Weigh gammon and calculate cooking time, allowing 20 minutes per 450g plus 20 minutes.

Place gammon in a large pan, add vegetables and cider with bay leaf and peppercorns.

Add sufficient cold water to cover gammon.

Bring slowly to boiling point.

Skim surface of impurities, with a draining spoon.

Cover pan with a tightly fitting lid and simmer for half cooking time, approx 50 minutes.

Drain and wrap gammon in foil.

Retain stock and use in a soup or sauce for a separate occasion. (The stock can be cooled completely, packed and frozen for up to 2 months.)

Bake foil wrapped gammon, standing in a roasting tin in an oven pre-heated to 180C (160 fan), Gas 4 until 30 minutes before cooking time is complete.

Increase oven temperature to, 200C (180 fan), Gas 6.

Remove foil and rind from gammon.
Score fat into diamonds, spread with mustard and stud with cloves.
Sprinkle surface with Demerera sugar, pressing it on to the fat.
Return gammon to hot oven, for approx 15 minutes, until crisp and golden.

Serve warm or cold.

CHEDDAR CHEESE & BROCCOLI FLAN

Suitable for vegetarians
200g plain wholemeal flour
Salt and black pepper
100g butter, diced
350g broccoli, trimmed
3 large eggs
300ml fresh whole milk
100g Cheddar cheese, grated

You will need 1x 23cm flan tin, loose bottomed, if possible.

Pre-heat oven to 200C (180 fan), Gas 6.

Put flour, 2.5ml salt and butter into a food processor fitted with metal blade.

Process, until mixture resembles fine breadcrumbs.

Add 6/7 teaspoons cold water and process into a ball of dough.

Turn out onto a floured board and knead until smooth.

Roll out pastry and use to line a 23cm flan dish. Stand flan tin on baking sheet. Chill in fridge for 10-15 minutes. Prick base and sides with a fork.

Bake blind for 15-20 minutes, until lightly golden.

Roughly chop broccoli and cook in a little boiling water for about 4 minutes until just tender.

Drain well. Blot dry on kitchen paper, and arrange in flan case.

Reduce heat of oven to 190C (170 fan), Gas 5.

Whisk together the eggs, milk and a seasoning of salt and pepper.

Sprinkle cheese over broccoli.

Pour over milk mixture, carefully.

Bake for about 40 minutes until lightly set.

Best served warm.

COLESLAW WITH BLUE CHEESE DRESSING

50g Stilton blue cheese, rind removed
30ml mayonnaise, Hellmann's is good
5ml lemon juice
150g natural yoghurt (not set variety)
Salt and black pepper
1 head fennel, finely shredded
225g red cabbage, very finely shredded
1 eating apple, cored and chopped leaving skin on
50g sultanas
3 spring onions, white part finely chopped

Prepare dressing. Put Stilton cheese, mayonnaise and lemon juice into a food processor fitted with the metal blade.

Whizz until smooth. Turn into mixing bowl. Gradually beat in yoghurt and season to taste.

Put shredded fennel, red cabbage, apple, sultanas and spring onion into a large salad bowl.

Pour over dressing and toss until well coated. Cover and chill until ready to serve.

BANOFFI PIE

75g butter
175g digestive biscuits, crushed
1x 397g can condensed milk
175g butter
175g caster sugar
2 bananas
Juice ½ lemon

To serve: whipped cream

You will need 1x20cm loose bottomed flan tin, lightly greased with a little of the butter.

In a large saucepan, melt butter. Stir in crushed digestive biscuits.
Press mixture onto base and sides of flan tin. Chill.

In a large, non-stick saucepan, combine condensed milk, butter and sugar. Stirring frequently, heat until sugar dissolves.

Boil for 5 minutes, stirring constantly to make a light, golden caramel. Pour into the biscuit case and leave to cool. Chill until firm.
Remove from flan tin.

Slice banana and sprinkle with lemon juice. Arrange over caramel.

Serve the pie with whipped cream.

MENU 21
Quick and Easy Supper
Serves 6
Some skill required: Ready in 40 minutes, approx.

* Chicken & Mushroom Risotto
* Griddled Pineapple with Blackberries

You may like to add a salad from one of the other menus.

Short grain pudding rice is cheaper than risotto rice and may be used instead.

Prepare and cook pineapple between courses.

I have included this simple supper menu which needs no timetable, as it is a useful speedy menu to have up your sleeve for various occasions. Once guests are assembled, simply prepare and cook risotto to serve.

CHICKEN & MUSHROOM RISOTTO
Smooth, creamy and very filling, this great recipe is made mostly from store cupboard ingredients..

Approximately 1.1litres chicken or vegetable stock
25g butter
2 tablespoons olive oil
1 large onion, finely chopped
2 cloves garlic, chopped
400g risotto rice
300ml dry cider
Salt and pepper
100g garlic and herb light cream cheese
225g button mushrooms, halved
Approx 225g left over roast chicken, diced, optional
2 tablespoons freshly chopped chives

In a large saucepan, heat the stock, and have it beside you as you work.

In a separate, large, non-stick saucepan heat butter and olive oil, until butter foams. Add onion, and fry gently for about 8 minutes, stirring frequently, until softened. Add garlic and continue to cook for 1 minute.

Add rice and turn the heat up. Continue to cook, stirring, for about 2 minutes, until rice turns translucent.
Add cider and cook, stirring, for another minute or so. Once cider has been absorbed, start to add the stock, a ladle full at a time.

Reduce heat and continue to add stock, a ladle full at a time, stirring and allowing each addition to be absorbed before you add another one.

After about 15 minutes, all the stock should be absorbed and the rice should be cooked. Check rice is soft but with a slight bite. If necessary, add a little boiling water.

Check seasoning, adding salt and pepper, if necessary.

Remove from heat and gradually stir in cream cheese, to melt.

Stir in mushrooms, and cooked chicken with the chives. Set aside for 2 minutes. Serve.

GRIDDLED PINEAPPLE WITH BLACKBERRIES

75g Demerara sugar
Juice 1 orange
2 tablespoons Grand Marnier or Cointreau, optional
1 pineapple
225g blackberries, or ripe plums, halved and stoned
To serve: vanilla ice cream

Put sugar, orange juice and 2 tablespoons water into a saucepan.

Bring slowly to the boil, stirring over a medium heat, to ensure sugar has dissolved. Simmer for 2 minutes. Set aside, stirring in liqueur, if using.

Peel pineapple and slice into wedges or rounds.

Place on hot griddle pan or pre-heated clean BBQ rack and cook for about 2 minutes each side, until lightly charred. Transfer to serving dish and add

blackberries or plums.

Serve warm, with the syrup poured over, accompanied by vanilla ice cream.

Recipe Index

Starters
Asian Style Smoked Salmon with Bean Sprout & Coriander Salad	19
Butternut Squash & Onion Soup	23
Carrot & Parsnip Soup	37
Chicken Liver Pâté	67
Garlic Mushrooms	16
Mussels with Garlic & Cream	53
Parma Ham with Pear & Dolcelatta	29

Main Courses
Beef Lasagne	53
Carbonara, Easy	71
Cheddar Cheese & Broccoli Flan	92
Chicken & Broccoli Bake	20
Chicken Fajitas, Cajun	77
Chicken & Mushroom Risotto	94
Chilli Con Carne with Guacamole & Garlic Bread	49
Cider Baked Gammon	91
Easy Carbonara	71
Fish Pie with Salmon, Prawns & Dill	45
Herbed Roast Shoulder of Lamb	41
Hungarian Goulash with Jacket Potatoes	30
Lamb Hot Pot with Sweet Potato Mash	67
Lamb Tagine	87
Marinated Tuna	23
Oven-Fried Indian Chicken	83
Pork & Chorizo Stew	58
Roast Belly of Pork	63
Salmon, Whole Baked	57
Sausage Casserole	73
Sesame Salmon with Roast Tomatoes & Noodles	33
Spiced Rack of Lamb with Red Wine Gravy & Butternut Squash Purée	16
Spicy Shepherd's Pie	38
Sweet Potato, Mozzarella & Pesto Tart	81

Bread
Garlic Bread	48
Naan Bread	84
Soda Bread	82

Vegetable Dishes
Buttered New Potatoes with Herbs	15
Buttery Cabbage with Caraway Seeds	64
Cauliflower & Broccoli	44
Couscous with Lemon, Coriander & Sultanas	86
Mange Tout & Carrots with Sage & Lemon Butter	42
Mashed Potatoes	64
New Potatoes	22
Potato Dauphinois	74
Roast Carrots & Courgettes	39
Roasted Roots	21
Roast New Potatoes with Salsa	42
Steamed Broccoli & Asparagus	70
Stuffed Mushrooms	26
Swede & Carrot Crush	74

Salads
Ciabatta Bread Salad	54
Coleslaw with Blue Cheese Dressing	93
Dressed Mixed Salad	31
Easy Guacamole	78
Minty Little Gem & Tomato Salad	84
Red & Green Coleslaw	26
Salad with Feta Cheese	34
Spinach & Avocado Salad	59

Desserts
Banoffi Pie	93
Cherry Clafoutis	79
Chocolate Biscuit Cake	71
Chocolate Mousse	50
Crème Brulée	75
Decadent Chocolate Cake	46
Easy Apple Tarts	50
Eton Mess	31
Flapjack & Raspberry Trifle	21
Fruits in Kirsch	83
Griddled Pineapple with Blackberries	95
Jelly Trifles	82
Lemon Cheesecake	69
Lemon Meringue Pie	88
Lemon Syllabub with Raspberries	17
Lemon, Raspberry & Kiwifruit Pavlova	60
Mango, Melon & Ginger Fruit Salad	39
Plum & Blackberry Crumble with Brazil Nuts	27
Poached Pears in Fruity Tea	27
Sliced Melon with Blackberries	70
Steamed Syrup Sponge	65
Strawberries Dipped in Chocolate	34
White Chocolate Cheesecake with Strawberries, Baked	43
Zabaglione	55